AF254823

Life in a South Texas Colonia

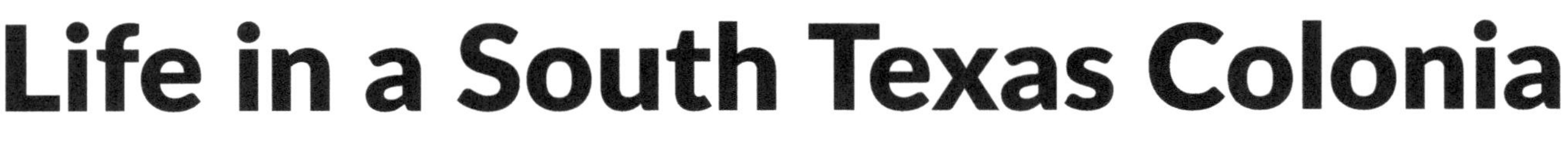

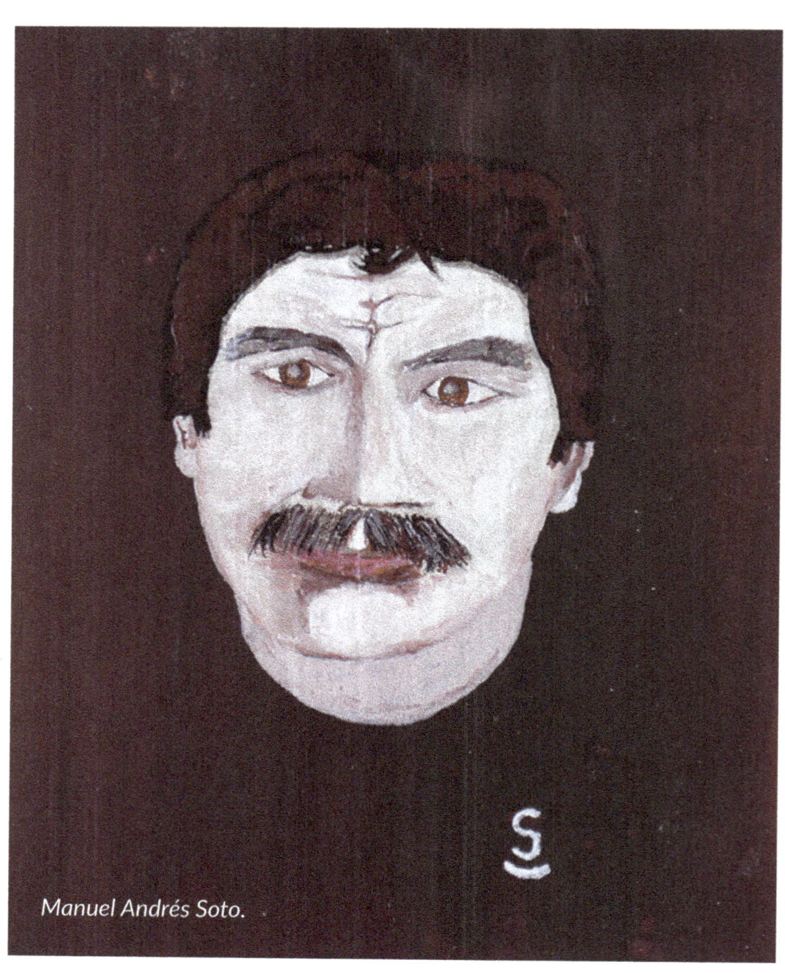

Manuel Andrés Soto.

Life
in a South Texas
Colonia

Manuel Andrés Soto

Artwork photographed by Raúl Baez
and Sarah Elizabeth Soto

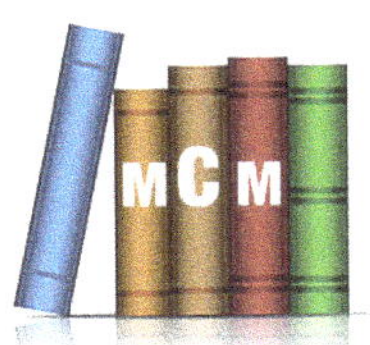

MCM Books, March 2017

Published in the United States by MCM Books, Corpus Christi, Texas.

ISBN: 978-0-9967473-1-8

Library of Congress Control Number: 2017930086

Dedication

This book is dedicated to my son Andrés Gabriel Soto who was the inspiration for the artwork and anecdotes in the book. His image, depicting *EL Tejano*, adorns the cover.

It is also dedicated to my loving brother David I. Soto who passed away on February 8, 2014. David was truly a servant of the Edroy-Odem communities in many ways. He especially loved to serve the youth and was very active in the schools and Little League baseball. Many remember him as the voice of the Odem Owls, as he was an announcer at their home games.

Foreword

Soto uses mainly acrylic paints and pine or cedar planks to create his impressionistic folk art. His subject matter focuses on various aspects of Tejano culture.

Manuel Andrés "Andy" Soto has had a lifelong fascination with art. He has also had a deep appreciation for his Tejano roots in South Texas. It has been his dream for a number of years to share with his only child, Andrés Gabriel Soto, his roots in a South Texas colonia. He chose his love for art to express to his son his love for his cultural roots as a Tejano son of the soil.

Manuel Andrés Soto grew up in Edroy, Texas, and graduated from nearby Odem High School in Odem, Texas. He earned a BA in biology in 1993 and an MA in biology in 1996, both from Texas A&M University-Kingsville. In 2001, he earned a PhD in Coastal Sciences from the Gulf Coast Research Laboratory at the University of Southern Mississippi. He is currently an Associate Professor of Biological and Health Sciences at Texas A&M University-Kingsville, where he has authored several peer-reviewed manuscripts in international scientific journals.

But this book is about his art, his family, and his culture.

Soto uses mainly acrylic paints and pine or cedar planks to create his impressionistic folk art. His subject matter focuses on various aspects of Tejano culture. His inspiration is his childhood growing up in a small rural town in San Patricio County. Edroy was no more than a colonia. Many colonias are located on the border with Mexico, although they can and are found in many other counties throughout South Texas. The Texas Secretary of State describes a typical colonia as "a residential area that may lack some of the most basic living necessities, such as potable water and sewer systems, electricity, paved roads, and safe and sanitary housing."

While Soto's neighborhood may have been lacking in amenities, his home provided a solid foundation for learning. Soto was the youngest in a family of eleven children. His parents provided everything the children needed to grow up to be successful adults. Like most of their neighbors, they did not have financial riches, but their immediate and extended family and neighbors more than made up for the lack of money. They had a roof over their heads, warm clothing, plenty to eat, and most of all a never ending source of love.

Soto has returned to his rural roots, although in many ways he never left them. Today he lives in a small ranch near Odem he calls the "Rockin S Land and Cattle". All of his artwork is signed with the ranch brand **S**. Soto, his son, other relatives, and friends have been building a retro barn house on the ranch, which serves as his art studio and gallery for all the original paintings appearing in this book.

It is at Rockin S that Soto can sit and reminisce about his growing up in a colonia. He is also freed from the many modern day distractions that can be a plague on an artist's creative mind. It is here that he remembers, takes brush in hand, and transfers those rich memories into art for the rest of the world to enjoy. With the publication of this book, the rest of the world can indeed enjoy Soto's extraordinary gift.

Those who grew up in South Texas in the 1940s through 1980s, whether in a colonia or in a small town or out in the country, will quickly relate to his art and the short vignettes that accompany each piece. Who can forget their outhouse? Or going to the *pizcas* atop of the neighbor's large *troca*. Or eating *sandia* on the porch and spitting out the seeds. Or taking your *asadon* to go to the *desahijé*. Or getting some *queso del condado*.

So many memories, so much joy.

How—you may ask—can so much joy be present in poverty.

Because most people in those conditions did not consider themselves *pobres*. They rarely, if ever, saw the *ricos*. All they knew were *pobreza* and so to them they lived like everyone they knew lived. *Y además*, they had their families. That was all they needed. A father and mother were always present. And in

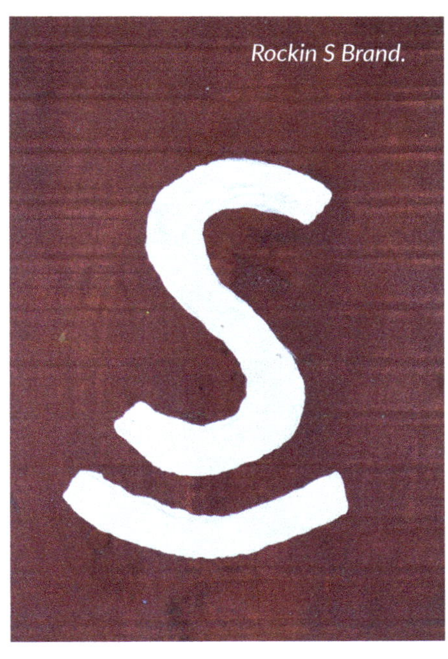

many instances so were the *abuelos*, *tíos* and *tías*, *primos y primas* and the *vecinos* who were like family.

Soto's humble beginnings were foundational for his success in academia, and they were equally motivational in his quest to honor his culture in art. While his beginnings were crucial to his success, they were inspirational to his art.

Fortunately, everyone can now partake of this joy. With the publication of his first book, Soto has generously provided us with reproductions of his paintings that will bring back a rush of memories to his readers. You will have something you can sit down in your recliner to show you grandchildren and tell them about their ancestors and how they lived, or take outside to your patio and enjoy it with your own sons and daughters while you have something *en las brasas*, or take it to the ranch to share with your aging parents. And if one or more of the paintings strikes your fancy, you can order a print from the artist.

Truly, Andy Soto has captured not only history but personal memories shared by a wide range of people with Tejano roots. It is yet another important addition to your Tejano book library to preserve our South Texas history and culture. 🄂

Alfredo E. Cárdenas
South Texas Historian
and Author

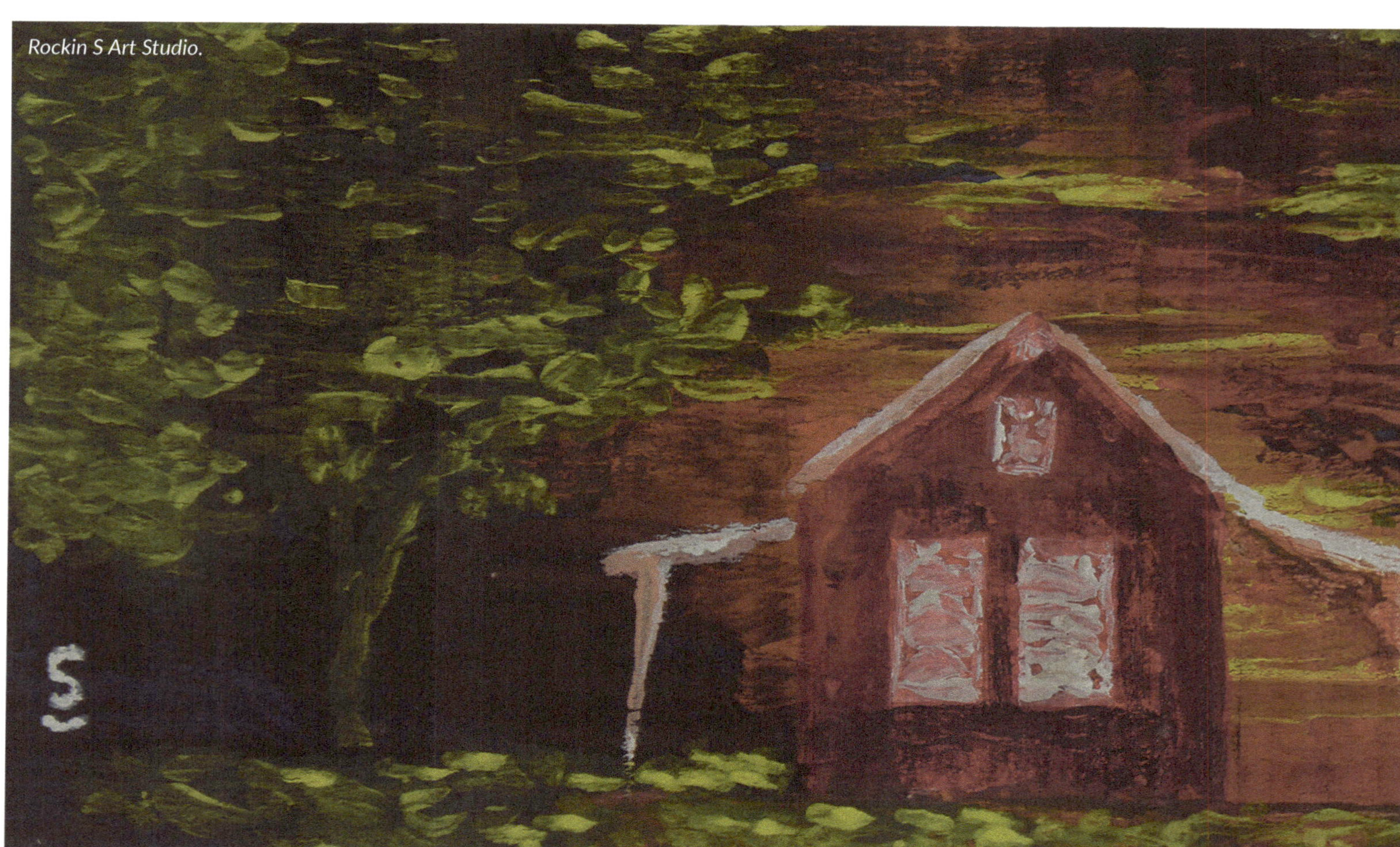

Preface

Human populations converge

Approximately 15,000 years ago, humans first entered the un-inhabited land that became known as the Americas. These first visitors came from the west and were nomadic people that eventually expanded their presence throughout all areas of their new discovery. Through the centuries they established great civilizations that developed advances in culture, science, mathematics, art, and other fields.

By contrast, it was 500 years ago that the first Europeans—known to the natives as the "children of the sun"—arrived in this "new world". The Earth's human population from the east and the west converged. Sadly, for the first Americans, this encounter was the beginning of the eventual devastation of their civilizations and population. Very few indigenous Americans exist today.

The confluence of what today are referred to as Native Americans and the Spaniards resulted in a new group of people commonly known as mestizos. As a result of the genetic material of many different Native American groups, this new ethnic group took on different cultural characteristics.

The mestizo population is thriving and is found throughout the Americas. In the United States, these new group of people are variously known as Latinos, Chicanos, and Hispanics.

Mestizos that reside in Texas are commonly known as Tejanos and are most highly concentrated in

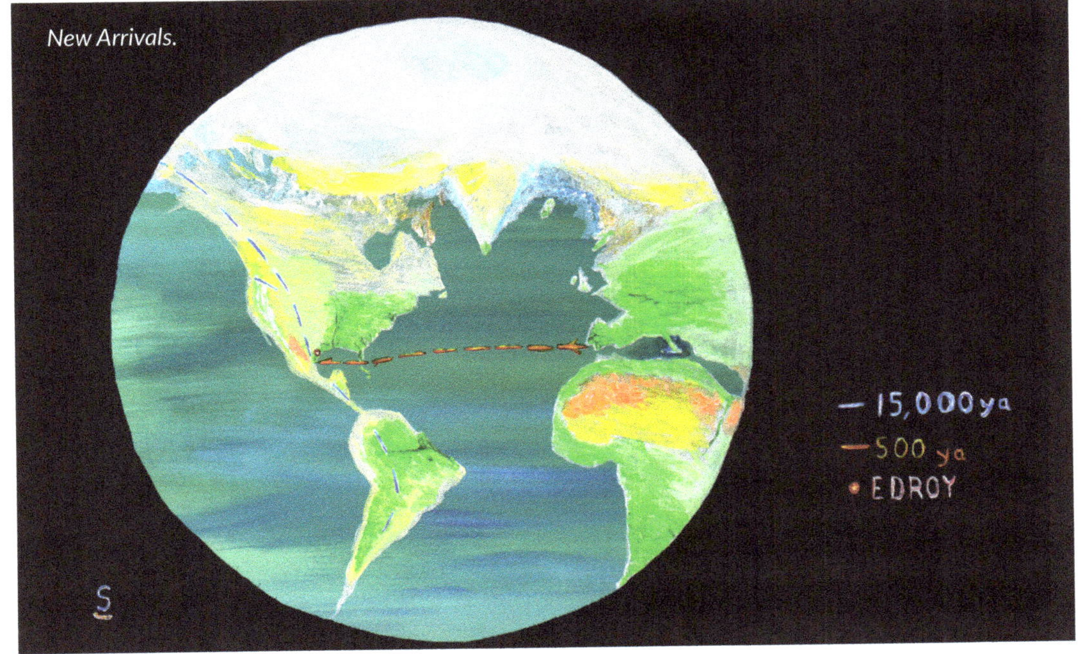

> *The confluence of what today are referred to as Native Americans and the Spaniards resulted in a new group of people commonly known as mestizos.*

the southern and western parts of the state, bordering with Mexico, as well as in the state's major metropolitan centers. Tejanos speak English, Spanish, and Spanglish, a blend of Spanish and English.

South Texas

Prior to the introduction of sheep, cattle, and horses, South Texas was an immense grassland. The introduction of this livestock by the Spaniards changed this landscape to brush land, mostly of mesquite and huisache. Movement of livestock and the subsequent spread of seed through the digestive tract of these animals resulted in mesquite and huisache trees expanding their range northward and becoming the dominant type of trees in this area.

In the early 1900s, railroads began to crisscross this landscape. In addition to transporting people, the railroads carried cattle, produce, cotton, and other goods from Texas fields to northern and eastern markets, as well to ports throughout the United States for shipment to foreign markets. The demand for these products grew rapidly, and farming communities began to sprout throughout South Texas. Some of these smaller communities, called colonias (subdivisions), lacked amenities and were predominantly populated by Tejanos.

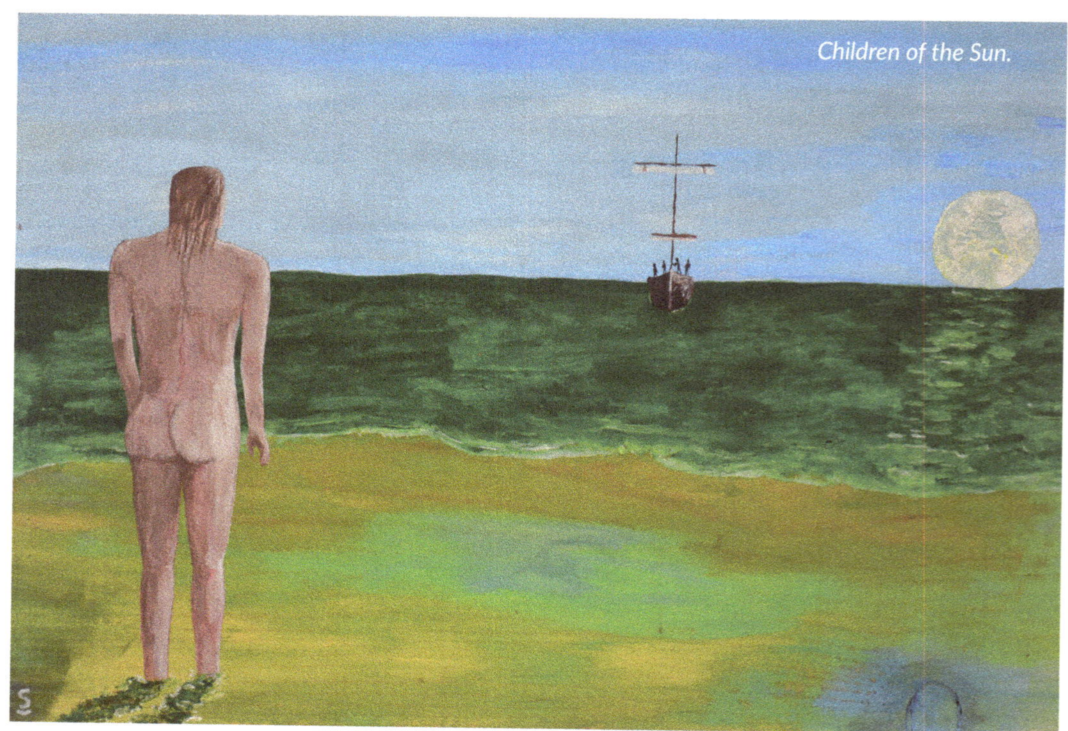

Edroy, a Texas Colonia

Edroy, located about ten miles northwest of Corpus Christi and 100 miles southeast of San Antonio in the South Texas county of San Patricio, is one of these colonias. The hamlet was developed in 1913 by Ed Cubage and Roy Miller, from whom it took its name. The town was later subdivided into small residential plots and sold to poor Tejano farmworkers. The population of Edroy never exceeded 500, and has mostly been at about 200.

Edroy, like other South Texas towns, soon became an thriving agricultural community. The area attracted thousands of seasonal workers, mostly Tejanos, to work in agricultural jobs. The Tejanos cleared fields for farming and harvested, packaged, and loaded mesquite wood, vegetables, and other goods onto railroad cars for transport to northern markets. Already located on a major highway between San Antonio and the Port of Corpus Christi, in the 1920s Edroy also gained a railroad station. Several vegetable packing warehouses also opened adjacent to the railroad tracks.

In addition to the packing warehouses, the town boasted a cotton gin and two grain elevators that stored sorghum and maize. Cattle ranches surrounded Edroy, and the town's feedlot processed more than 25,000 cattle during

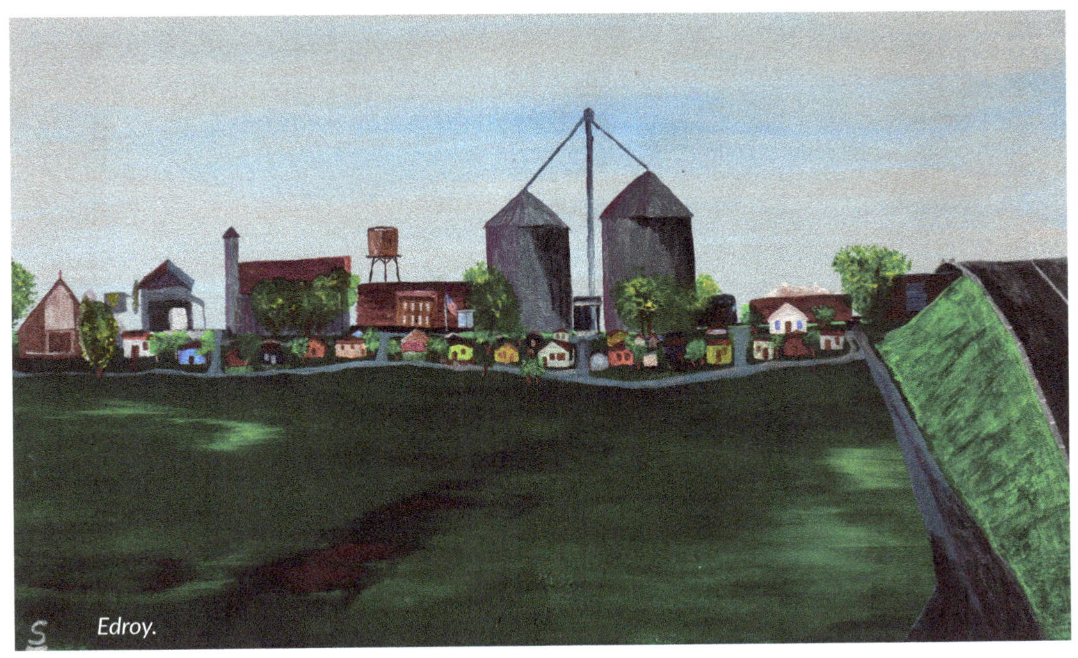

Edroy.

peak production in the 1980s. Almost all the people working in these enterprises were Tejanos, however the agricultural land and businesses were owned by Anglos.

Early housing in Edroy can best be described as one and two room shacks called *casitas* (little houses) that their Tejano owners progressively enlarged and improved through the years. The residents relied on wells powered by windmills, and later electric pumps, to obtain water. Few *casitas* had interior plumbing, and outhouses were used until the 1980s. Prior to the mid-1900s when natural gas became available to heat homes and for cooking, these *casitas* were warmed by wood, which was also used for cooking. Modern cooling systems were not used extensively in homes until late in the 1900s.

In its early years, several stores operated in Edroy along with three gasoline stations, all of which are no longer in business. In 1934, the Catholic diocese of Corpus Christi established Our Lady of Guadalupe Mission, which is still active. In 1950 the Post Office,—which had been closed for many years—reopened and remains in operation today. The town's children attend school in nearby Odem, which is part of the Odem-Edroy Independent School District.

Until the late 1900s, several large families, including the Sotos, comprised the permanent residents of Edroy. This is the story of the tens of thousands of Tejano families, wherever they may be in the diaspora, as experienced by the Soto family from Edroy. S

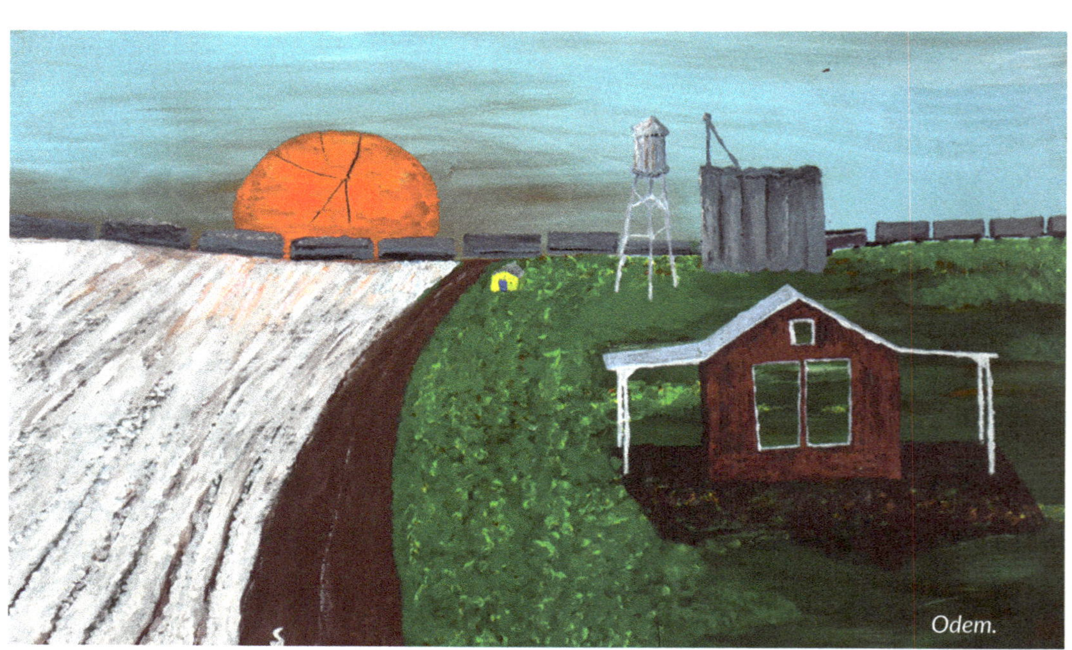

La familia Soto
(The Soto family)

Mis abuelos paternos (My paternal grandparents)

My fraternal grandparents were my *abuelito* (grandpa) Donato Soto (1892-1936) and my *Abuelita* (grandma) Manuela Palos Soto (1896-1978). My grandfather was born in Duval County, Texas and grandmother in Mier, Tamaulipas, México. Their presence in South Texas took a route very familiar to many South Texas Tejanos. Mier is the genealogical cradle of many South Texas Tejanos. My ancestors would have taken the Camino Real from Mier to Goliad via the ranchos, that dotted the road, including many in Duval County.

They were married when he was nineteen and she was thirteen. Five of their sons reached adulthood, including my father Amando P.

Their presence in South Texas took a route very familiar to many South Texas Tejanos.

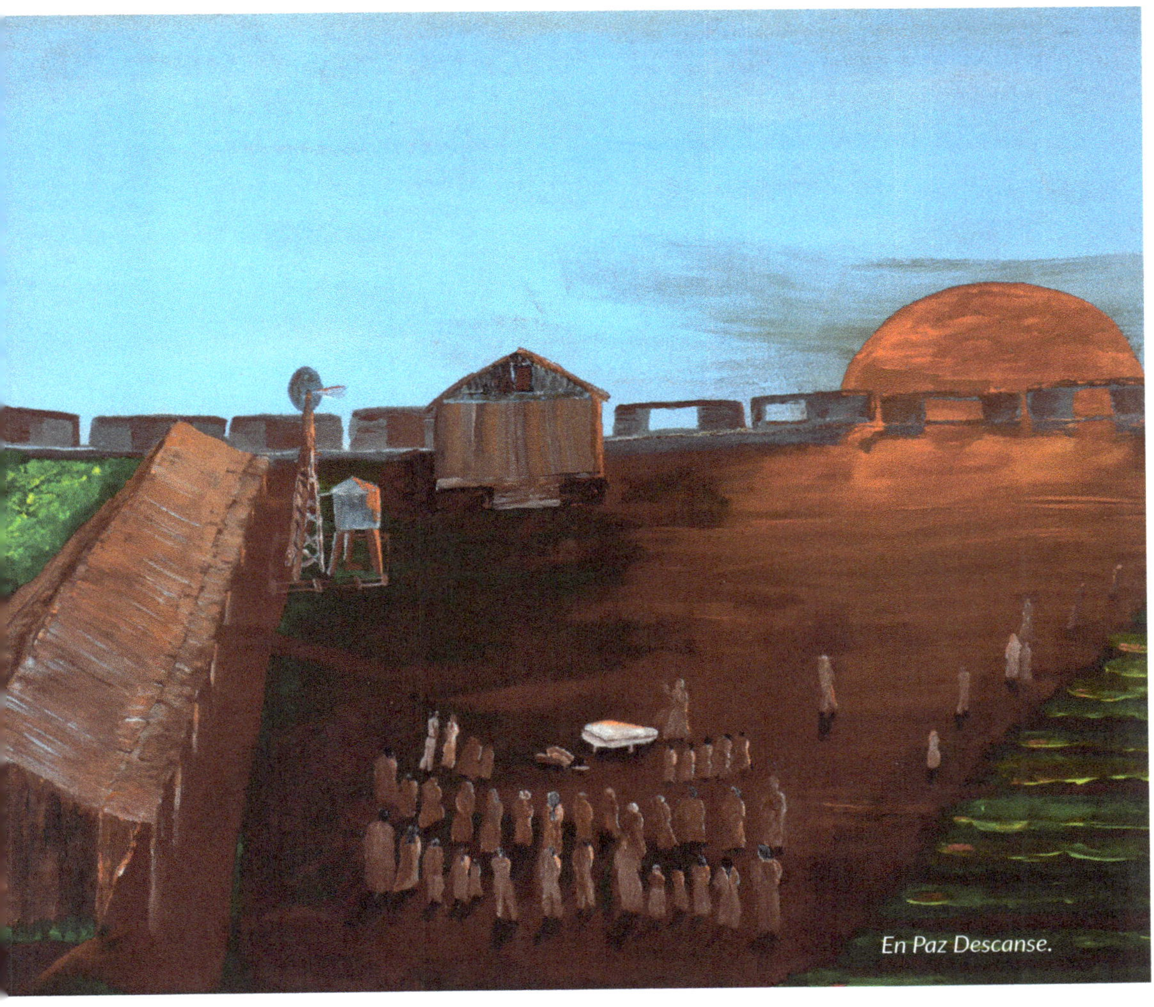

Soto (1924-94). For a time in the 1930s my grandparents lived three miles northwest of Edroy, Texas in San Patricio County at a ranch the locals called "*el rancho de en medio*" (the ranch in the middle).

My grandfather was a vaquero and a farmworker.

Abuelito was a debonair and handsome man who enjoyed an occasional drink and liked to gamble. He was popular with the ladies, except of course with my *Abuelita* who did not take kindly to his romantic adventures. At sunset, he usually rode his horse *Chango* to neighboring towns to gamble.

On April 12, 1936, after one of his outings, he rode back to *el rancho de en medio* quite sick. He needed help dismounting and called *Abuelita* to come help him into the room of the row housing where they lived. She took off his boots. He gasped for every breath, and foamed at the mouth. *Abuelita* sent for the doctor who told her that *abuelito* was poisoned. Two days later, my grandfather died a painful, agonizing death.

Abuelita, his sons, and the rest of his family, as well as his friends and neighbors, pointed to one of his mistresses, who lived in a nearby town, as the culprit for his poisoning. The family and neighbors spent many hours *platicando* (conversing) about and

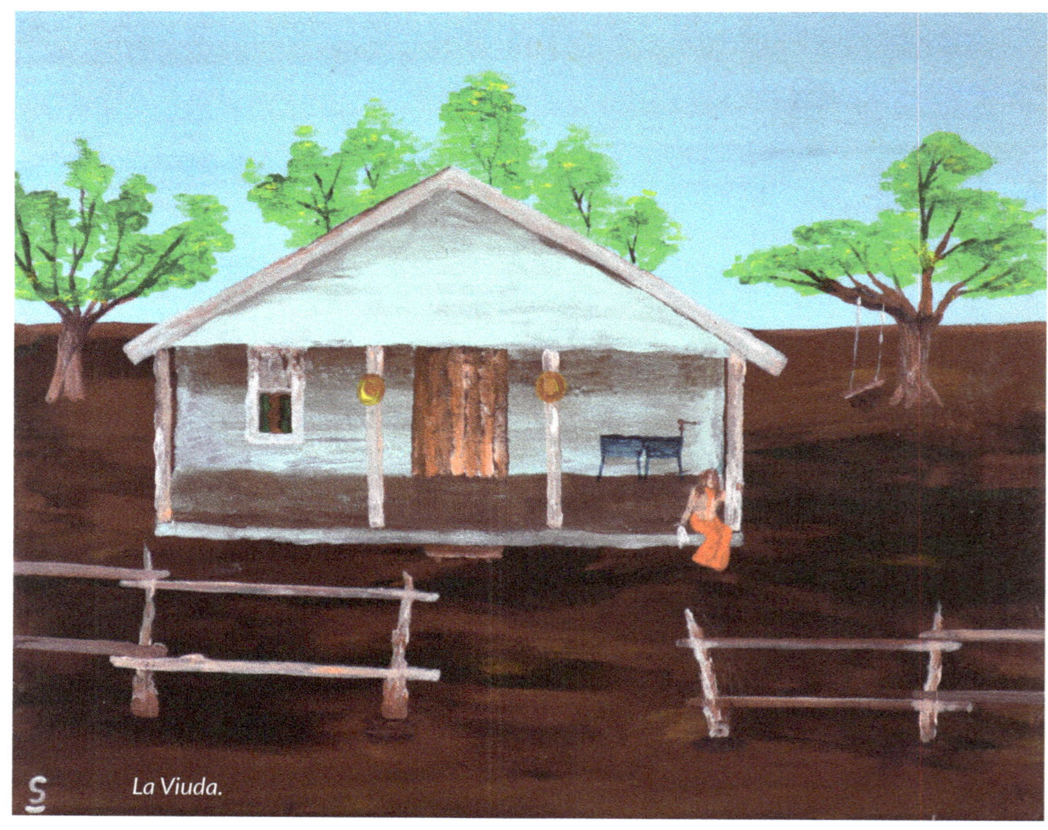

La Viuda.

believing that he was poisoned to death by his mistress. Many living family members still think the mistress poisoned him.

Despite this family lore, the doctor wrote in the death certificate that the cause of death was tetanus, which is a bacterial infection usually introduced into the body by a cut or a scratch. Working as a vaquero and farmhand there were many opportunities to introduce the bacteria into grandpa's body. Tetanus causes muscles, including those responsible for breathing, to stop working. This could explain the gasping for air and foaming at the mouth. One of the first symptoms of tetanus is lockjaw. Grandpa most likely died an excruciating and painful death from a tetanus infection.

But why did the doctor tell *Abuelita* her husband was poisoned? Doctors, even today, say that a patient's blood is poisoned when they have a bacterial infection that spreads throughout the entire body, or when certain toxins are building up in the blood because of kidney failure.

Grandpa was a gambler and had a mistress, but his mistress probably did not kill him. In the translation from English to Spanish, grandma probably misunderstood the doctor's diagnosis. *Que en paz descanse* (May he rest in peace).

Recently widowed, *Abuelita* bought two narrow lots in Edroy in about 1940. She paid $54 for them and built a small two-room house (14 x 24 ft.) on one of the lots. She never remarried and raised her five sons and two grandchildren in this house.

Abuelita was young when she was widowed and, according to one source, she did have male acquaintances. However, most that knew her say that she disliked men. She took extreme measures to repel potential suitors. For example, she made her oldest son smoke tobacco at a very young age, so the tobacco smell permeated in the house at all times. The smell of smoke was a sure sign that a man was living there. She also hung a man's sombrero at the entrance of her house.

Mis abuelos maternos (My maternal grandparents)

My maternal grandparents were Fructoso Carranza (1896-1974) and Elena Guerra Carranza (1895-1939). He was born in, Tamaulipas, México, and she was born in Helena in Karnes County, Texas. They married in the early 1900s and had nine children between 1919-34. Their sixth child was my mother, Mária de la Luz Carranza (1928-2002).

My grandmother Elena died of tuberculosis in November 1939 when my mother was eleven. One month later, her father, and my great-grandfather, Sabas Guerra, died of tuberculosis as well. After their deaths, the doctor told grandpa to burn all their belongings and take his family elsewhere. They relocated about 70 miles south of Helena to Sinton, Texas.

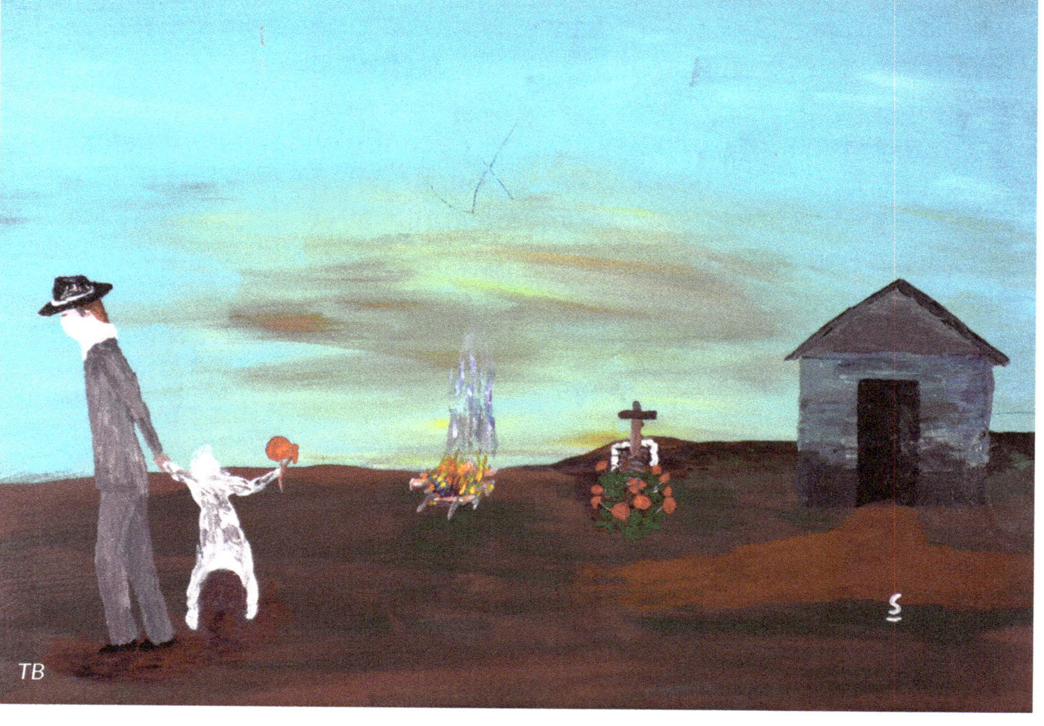

Mis padres (My parents)

My father Amando Soto, who we called *Papi* (daddy), was born in Beeville, Texas and was raised in *el rancho de en medio* and Edroy. He met our mother, whom we called *Mami* (mommy), Mária de la Luz Carranza, in 1944. They were married shortly thereafter. He was nineteen and she was fourteen. They had eleven children, six boys and five girls. The oldest was born in 1945 and the youngest in 1969. I am the youngest.

In Edroy, as was the case in many Tejano families of that time, large families of eight to twelve children were common.

Abuelita Soto sold one of the two plots she bought in Edroy to my father and over the years he built three houses on this corner plot. Houses in Edroy weathered quickly, and my father built new houses adjacent to the old worn-out ones. As soon as the new house had a roof and some walls they moved in. Each house was built larger to accommodate the growing family. My father started building the last house in the late

1960s and the family moved in 1970. This house still stands, and is the only house I lived in while growing up.

My mother can best be described by her immense love for her children, her commitment to her children's education, her devout Catholic faith, and most importantly passing that faith to her children. My mother's determination that her children receive an education was probably emboldened as a result of her own education being interrupted early in her life because of her mother's illness and death. Before she died, *Abuelita Elena* was sending all of her children to school. As a result of her untimely death, many of my mom's older siblings were literate in English, but my mother was not.

My mother experienced the difficulty of living without a formal education. She always needed a translator to communicate with the ever-growing English-speaking community, including doctors, nurses, and teachers. When her kids were going to school in the 1950s through the 1980s there were very few bilingual professionals.

Mami could not do some of the simple things that mothers do with their children. She never read to us; we read to her. She could not correct our homework. She did, however, know what a high mark looked like on report cards, and she took extreme measures to ensure that her kids knew that their number one priority in life was to get a good education.

I strayed from that understanding many times, but in particular in the seventh grade when I was finally able to fulfill my ambition of playing interscholastic football. My dedication to football was my sole passion. That year I failed one class and barely passed another. In the 1980s, a student could fail one class and still pass to the next grade. After my mother saw the report card she put me on her version of "no pass no play". For me it was no pass, no play for a year!

If that was not bad enough, I was placed in special classes in a separate building. To get to that building I had to walk past the ridiculing football players yelling obscenities. Some of them threw a football in front of me as I walked.

My mother realized the importance of education early in her life and was determined that all her kids get educated. Dropping out of school was not an option and she expected all of us to go to college.

Although my mother did not have a formal education, she vicariously earned many degrees through her children. She managed to accumulate several diplomas that she proudly displayed on her living room wall. Her eleven children earned eleven high school diplomas and a total of fourteen

college or technical degrees,
including seven undergraduate
degrees, five postgraduate degrees
and two technical certifications.
One year before her death,
while very ill, she endured a

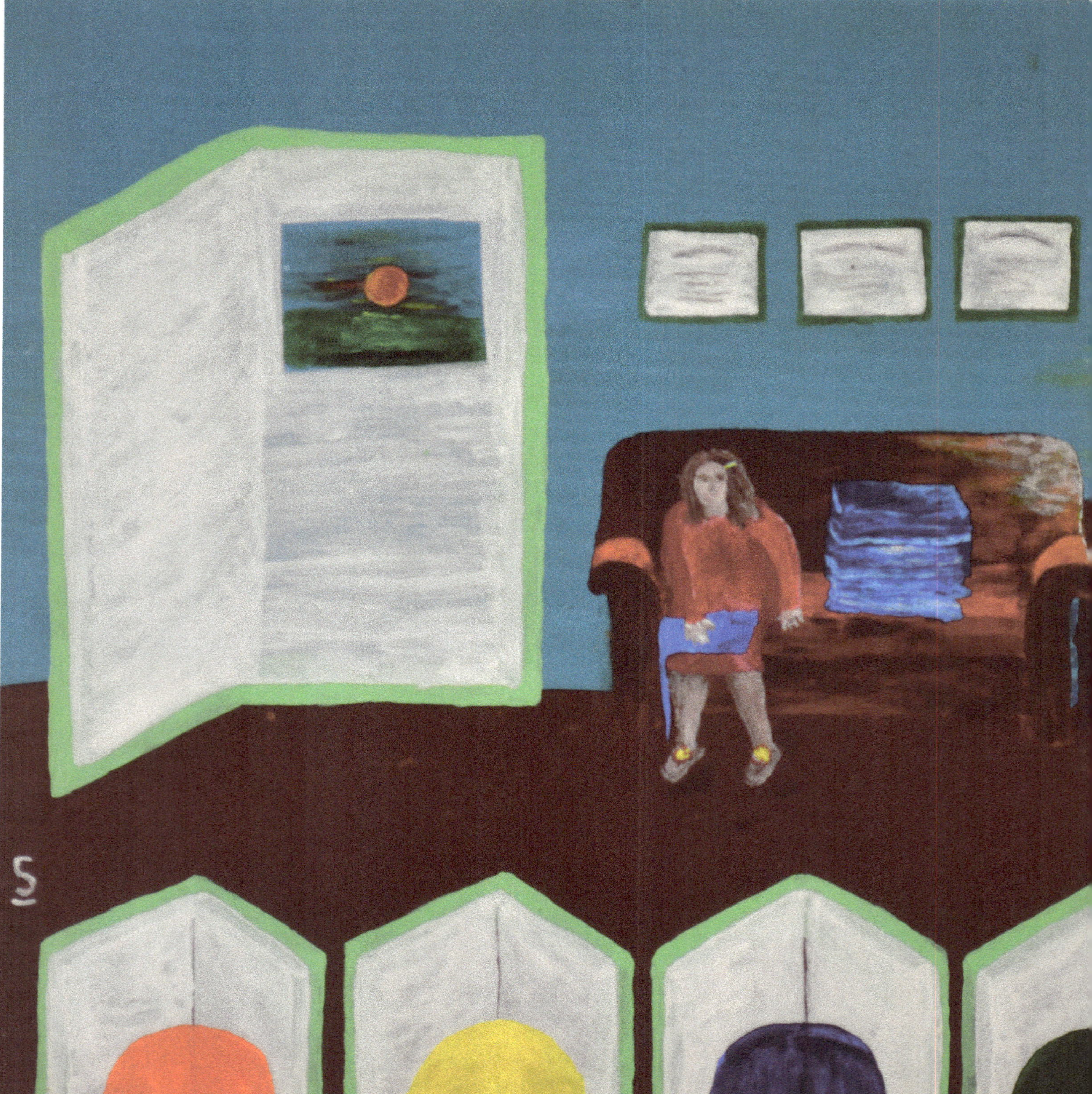

fourteen hour car trip to witness my hooding ceremony for my doctorate degree.

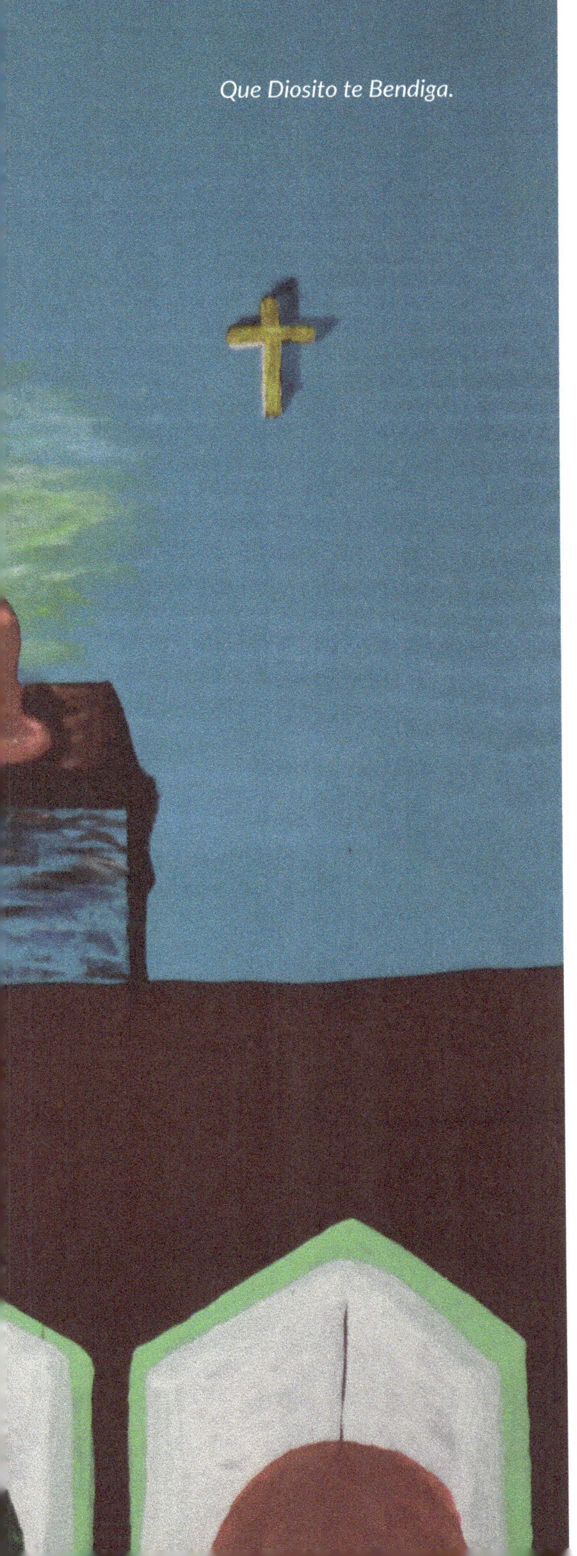

My mother had a deep commitment to her faith. She was a devout Roman Catholic. The family went to church every Holy Day of obligation, and her children received all the sacraments. We were infused with Catholicism every day of our lives. She had a crucifix hung by the main door. No one left her house without her saying, *que Diosito te bendiga* (may God bless you).

My father grew up during the depression and had a sixth grade education. He was drafted by the United States Army in 1945 during World War II, but never saw combat.

Papi had a loving and playful personality, but it could change in an instant. The extremes were so sudden and drastic that many of his children, including myself, believe he suffered from some form of bipolar disorder. It is difficult to describe such a dynamic personality in one anecdote. I have attempted to describe his personality from events described in several anecdotes and paintings in this book.

To describe my siblings and our many adventures or misadventures would take more time and space than I have in this book. Needless to say, like most families, we had many great times, lots of funs, some fights or quarrels, an occasional adventure, and a great deal of loving. Several of the paintings in this book deal with these experiences. 𝕊

My father grew up during the depression and had a sixth grade education. He was drafted by the United States Army in 1945 during World War II, but never saw combat.

Acknowledgments

A very special thank you goes to my son Andrés Gabriel Soto who was the inspiration for this book. It was a desire to preserve for him memories of his ancestors and their way of life that prompted me to do this art collection. Also a very special thanks to Raul Baez and my niece Sarah Elizabeth Soto who photographed all the artwork that appears in this book. Gabriel and Sarah also reviewed the manuscript.

I would also like to extend my sincere gratitude to Dr. Randy Powel, Patricia Horan, René Treviño, Dr. Saúl Sánchez, María Magdalena Soto, Anna Lisa Soto, Nathan Hinojosa, Ludy "Vinita" Ramírez García, Esperanza Benavidez, Ricardo Soto (La Toronja), Melissa Soto, Balbina Treviño, José Ricardo Treviño, Alfredo Martínez, Rosario Martínez, Amando Soto Jr., Gabriel Soto, Sonia Benavidez, Dalio Benavidez, Ismael Soto, Héctor Morín, Alfredo Morín, Marcelo Soto, Manuela Quintero Soto, Rubén Soto, Nora Nuñez-DeLeón, Juan Martínez, Joshua Martínez, Antonia V. Alvarez, Carla Jiménez, Inez Cedillo, Norma Soto, and David and Rosemary Cabrera.

Table of Contents

Illustrations

La pizca de algodón (cotton picking)

Until the late 1960s, and before the widespread use of mechanical cotton pickers, many Tejanos were hired to *pizcar algodón* (pick cotton). Many families in my hometown of Edroy picked cotton in nearby fields and on occasion migrated to other areas of Texas and the United States.

The head of the house took all his family to the cotton fields. Families were large, and often included three generations: grandparents, parents, and children of all ages. It was not unheard of for women expecting a child to be out on the fields along with the rest of her family. When migrating to other areas, families slept in some kind of row housing resembling abandoned Army barracks. These encampments had basic community kitchens, bathrooms, and showers. All family members, except the very young, picked cotton. The younger children waited at the head of the field.

Many families picked agricultural products throughout the summers until the mid 1970s. Most years, cotton picking started in August and was picked by October. Pickers worked from ten to twelve hours, Monday through Friday, and half days on Saturdays. Some families took their children out of school early to start working before the school year ended, and did not enroll them back in school until the next school year was well underway. When school opened for the fall session, children that were picking close to home generally picked cotton after school. Some children skipped school and picked cotton all day, a practice approved by parents and farmers, with the full knowledge of school administrators. Many parents, including mine, never allowed their children to miss school.

All cotton pickers stuffed cotton into canvas sacks as they dragged them through the *surcos* (rows) in the field. Using one of his legs, the picker packed the cotton tightly in the sack. Sacks were twelve to sixteen feet long. Children's sacks were six to ten feet long.

The pickers dragged the full sack to the weigh station where the weigh master, after weighing the sacks, recorded the amount of cotton picked by each individual. Another person, usually a large man, dumped the cotton unto a trailer, which was used to haul the cotton to the gin. If the ladies were too far from the weigh station, or if they were late in their pregnancy, someone dragged the sack to the weigh station for them.

A large tightly packed sack of cotton weighed from 100–125 pounds. A good picker picked around 500–700 pounds a day. Exceptional pickers, including ladies, picked 700-1,000 pounds per day.

Some children skipped school and picked cotton all day, a practice approved by parents and farmers, with the full knowledge of school administrators.

The most my sixteen year-old sister picked was 500 pounds. My thirteen year-old sister picked 300 pounds, and my brother, who was three-years younger, picked between 100–125 pounds.

Cotton pickers were paid by the pound; in the 1960s, the rate was 75¢-$1.25 per 100 pounds. Most earned $5 a day, but exceptional pickers could earn $10 a day. My sisters earned $5 and $3, respectively, and my brother $1.25, although they did not keep any money. Our family earned about $200 a week. In the mid-1960s, the minimum wage was $1.25/hour and a gallon of milk cost about 75¢-$1.

Earnings from the cotton picking were used to buy school clothes and supplies. The remainder helped sustain families for only part of the year. After the cotton picking season, adults found other jobs to make ends meet through the rest of the year.

In South Texas, the cotton picking season occurred during the two hottest months of the year. Daily high temperatures typically reached 95–100°F. Cotton fields are large, expansive, open areas with the only shade being under large trucks or the cotton trailers. During lunch, families sought refuge from the sun under these trucks or trailers. "A *él nomás le gusta estar abajo de la troca*, (He only wants to be under the truck)" was a common refrain for "lazy" cotton pickers who preferred the to remain in the *sombra* (shade).

The day's supply of drinking water was stored in the shaded areas as well. Although ice was added to the

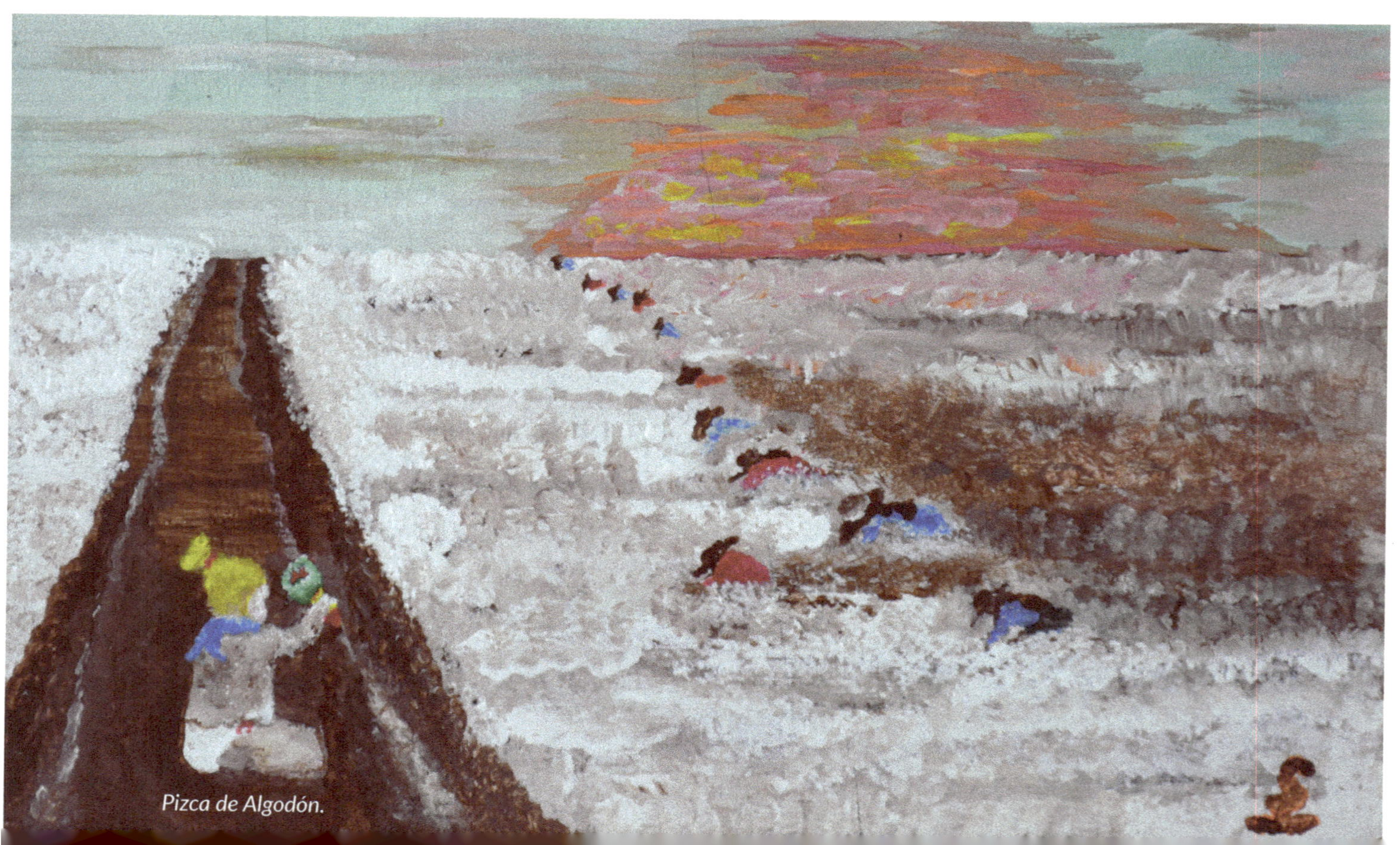

Pizca de Algodón.

water containers in the morning, it melted by midday. Workers had to drink warm water during the hottest part of the day.

Mechanized cotton pickers were in widespread use by the 1970s. I was born in 1969 and never picked cotton. I do remember playing at the head of a muddy field on one occasion in 1973 when the mechanical cotton pickers could not be used because of the mud, and the cotton from this field was given to my father. He took his family and some local cotton pickers to that field and enough cotton was picked to make one and a half bales of ginned cotton. A bale weighed about 500 pounds and in the 1970s sold for about $135.

Without a doubt, the Tejano mothers of these large families worked the hardest. They, my mother included, woke up at four in the morning, made breakfast and lunch, and packed that lunch for the entire family. After cleaning the kitchen, they joined their family in the fields to pick cotton the rest of the morning. At noon, they distributed lunches under the cotton trailers. After lunch, they picked cotton until about four in the afternoon and then made dinner. All this was done while caring for infants, toddlers, and older children. Amazingly, there were minimal complaints; in fact most mothers welcomed the opportunity to make the much-needed income. They were willing to endure the hard times for their families!

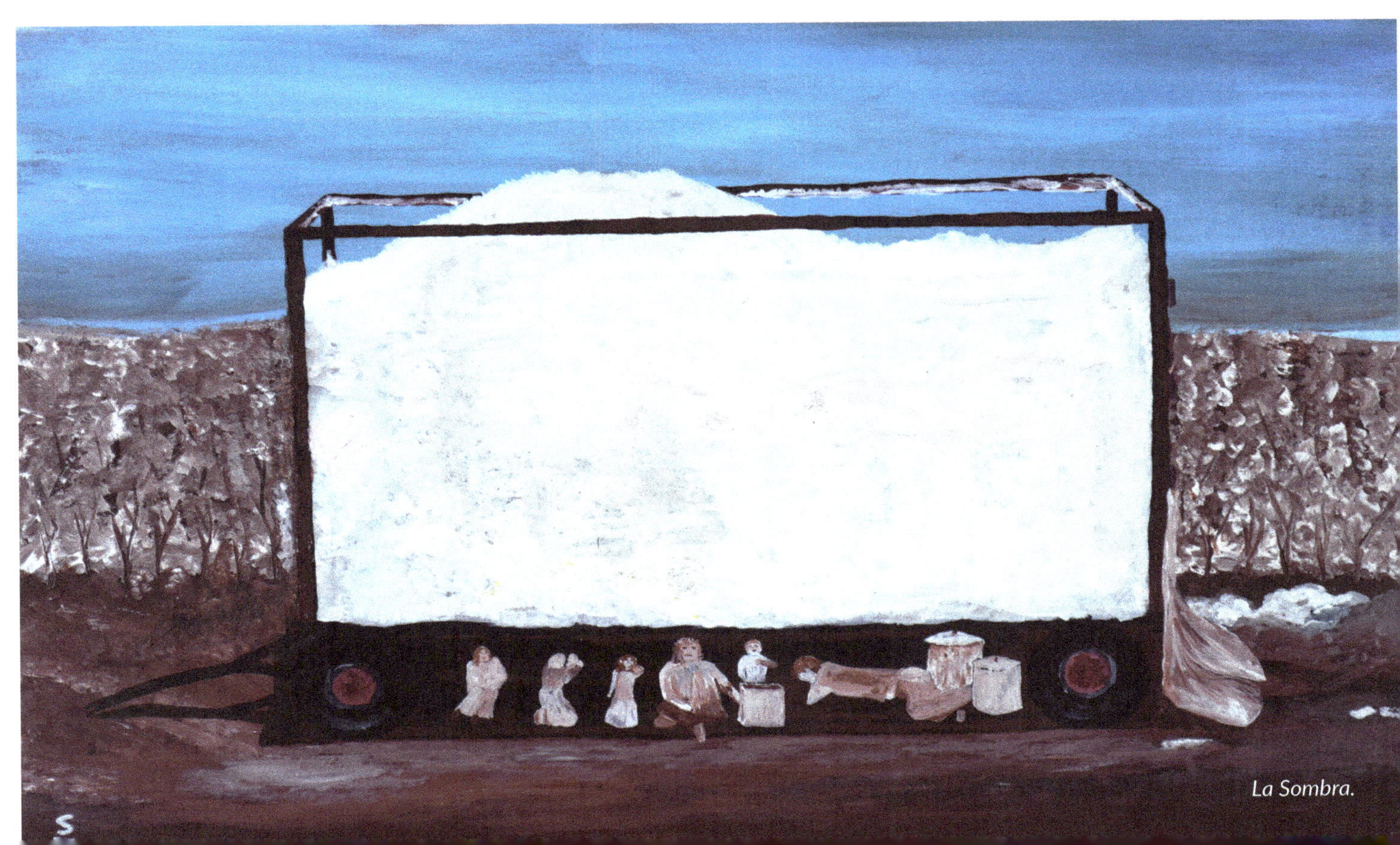

La Sombra.

La desenraizería (The uprooting)

The growing demand for agricultural products by northern markets in the early to mid-1900s, beckoned thousands of Tejanos to migrate to South Texas in general, and Edroy in particular, to work as farm laborers.

Because the landscape was converted from grassland to thick mesquite brush by grazing sheep and cattle, the primary job at this time was *la desenraizería*. This is back-breaking work that involves using a *talache* (mattock) and machete to clear land. The *talache* is about the size of an ax, but heavier, and is swung like an ax. It has a wooden handle and the steel head has an ax on one side and a flat hoe-shaped edge on the other side.

Workers used it to remove tree stumps. They got on their knees and using the hoe-side cleared leaf litter and dirt from around the roots and turned it to the ax side and cut away the stump. The owner of the land poked the ground with a metal rod to ensure there were no roots left.

La desenraizería is jarring and intensely physically demanding. Heavy machinery to do this work was not available. At one time or another, my grandfather and all of his sons, including my father, were *desenraizeros*.

The landowner paid *desenraizeros* by the day or by the cleared acre. In the early to mid-1900s, workers earned from 25¢ to $1 per day. By

La Desenraizería

comparison, the minimum wage in 1938 was 25¢ cents per hour.

Two events drastically changed the landscape in Edroy and throughout South Texas. First, grazing and migrating sheep and cattle transformed the grassland to brush. Second, the *desenraizeros*, most of which were Tejanos, using *talaches* and machetes, changed this landscape to farmland. 🅂

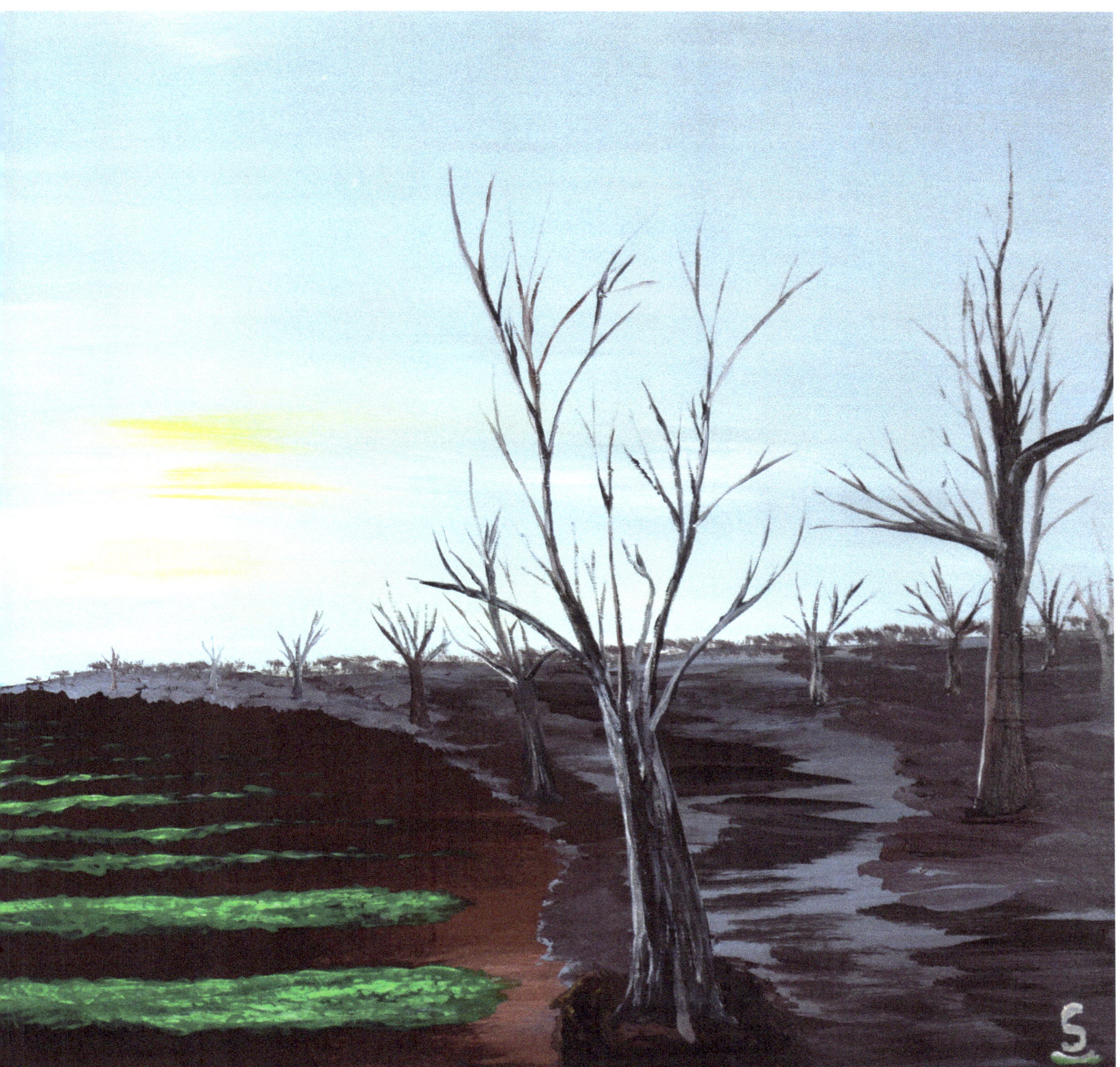

El elote (The corn)

Papi yelled, "*Ya está listo el elote. Súbanse a la pickup* (The corn is ready, get in the pickup). *Acuérdense, no más pizken los elotes que tienen los cabellos cafécitos* (Remember only to pick the corn with the light brown tassels.)"

Papi put burlap sacks in the back of his pickup and drove it to a corn field. If we had permission from the farmer to pick the field, we all got off and filled the sacks with ears of corn. If we did not have permission, dad drove to the field, stopped, and we jumped off and ran into the field, hopefully without getting caught. He then drove around for about ten minutes before going back to pick us up. We loaded the sacks onto the bed of the pickup as fast as possible and jumped in and *Papi* quickly drove back to the house.

At the house, we all helped shuck the ears and *Mami* put as many as she could into the largest pot, which she had ready with boiling water. We had corn on the cob for dinner *con mantequillita* (with a little butter) and not much else. Normally each person ate about five ears of corn. The record number eaten by one individual was 15.

This activity occurred about three times a year. **S**

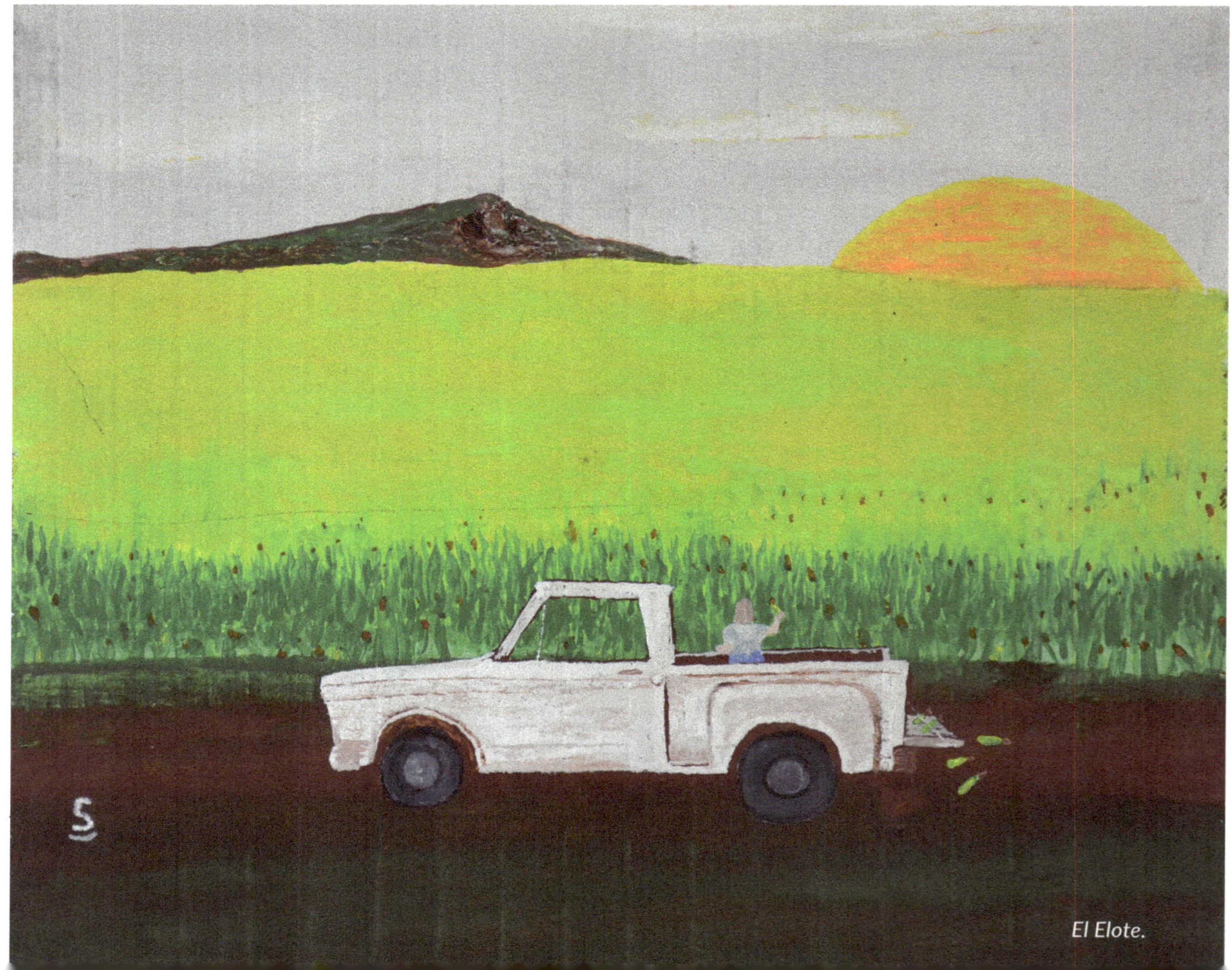

El Elote.

Working *en el* (on the) pipeline

In the summer of 1982, my father and my three older brothers—like many other Tejanos in South Texas—were working "*en el* pipeline" near Freer. Two brothers were living in Kingsville, where they were enrolled at Texas A&I University. The third brother working in the oilfields was still in high school. They met at the job-site in Freer on Monday, worked all week, and stayed in a local motel or in trailer houses.

They told stories of all the wildlife they saw while out in the *monte* (brush) around Freer. They spoke of deer, javelina, jack rabbits, and even rattlesnakes. I was a wildlife enthusiast from an early age and begged my parents to let me go to Freer. I was about 12-years-old and wanted to see the deer and javelina and anything else I encountered. They reluctantly agreed. Since the pipeline was nearly complete and the job was winding down, I was going in place of my brother who still lived at home.

I was so excited I could not sleep the night before. I remember it vividly. At about three in the morning I heard my dad *tomando café en la cocina* (drinking coffee in the kitchen). *Mami* was up too. She had all the burners on the stove going, cooking *taquitos* of *papas con huevo* (potato and eggs), *frijoles refritos* (refried beans), and pork chops on homemade flour tortillas. She was making breakfast, lunch, and extras for us, including my brothers that would join us from Kingsville. I helped pack the *taquitos* first in paper towels and then in aluminum foil and placed them in large brown bags. *Mami* poured "*café en el termo* (coffee in the thermos)" for *Papi*.

When we left the house at four thirty it was still dark. On the two and half hour drive to Freer I was wide awake and excited. Around dusk, we met up with my brothers and the rest of the work crew outside a gas station in Freer. My brothers immediately searched the car scavenging some of the breakfast taquitos and devoured them. I helped a couple of the workers fill the water jugs and put a block of ice in each one. As the foreman, my dad briefed the crew about their tasks although they already knew what to do. As we caravaned to the job site, the crew members jokingly inquired about me, asking "*quién es el ayudante nuevo* (who is the new helper)?"

The job site was still about thirty minutes away, deep in the brush, but on the way I saw lots of deer, herds of javelinas, jack rabbits everywhere, roadrunners dashing along the road, snakes crossing the road, armadillos scurrying along, skunks fearlessly walking around, and coyotes running in the distance. I had never seen so much wildlife in their natural habitat. It was all that *Papi* and my brothers described and more.

As soon as we got to the job-site, everyone took their places and started working. The tranquil, peaceful morning abruptly changed to the rumbling sound of the loud tractors, and even louder sound of my dad yelling orders.

My dad yelled at workers—whether they were family or not—in the same way. The work crew was composed of young and old, mainly Tejano and some Anglos. Delegating authority was never my dad's strength. He was in the ditches doing the work that could have been done by other crew members.

Everyone was working, and I was left by the pickup. I went for a couple of short walks, but my dad, fearing I may get bit by a snake, had given me strict orders not to go too far and "*mucho cuidado con las víboras* (be careful with the snakes)." I mainly stayed in the pickup with the windows rolled down. South Texas days were hot and dry in the summer, with daily high temperatures 100°F as the norm. My excitement quickly turned to boredom.

At noon my brothers came and got their lunch and ate with the rest of the work crew. My dad and I got

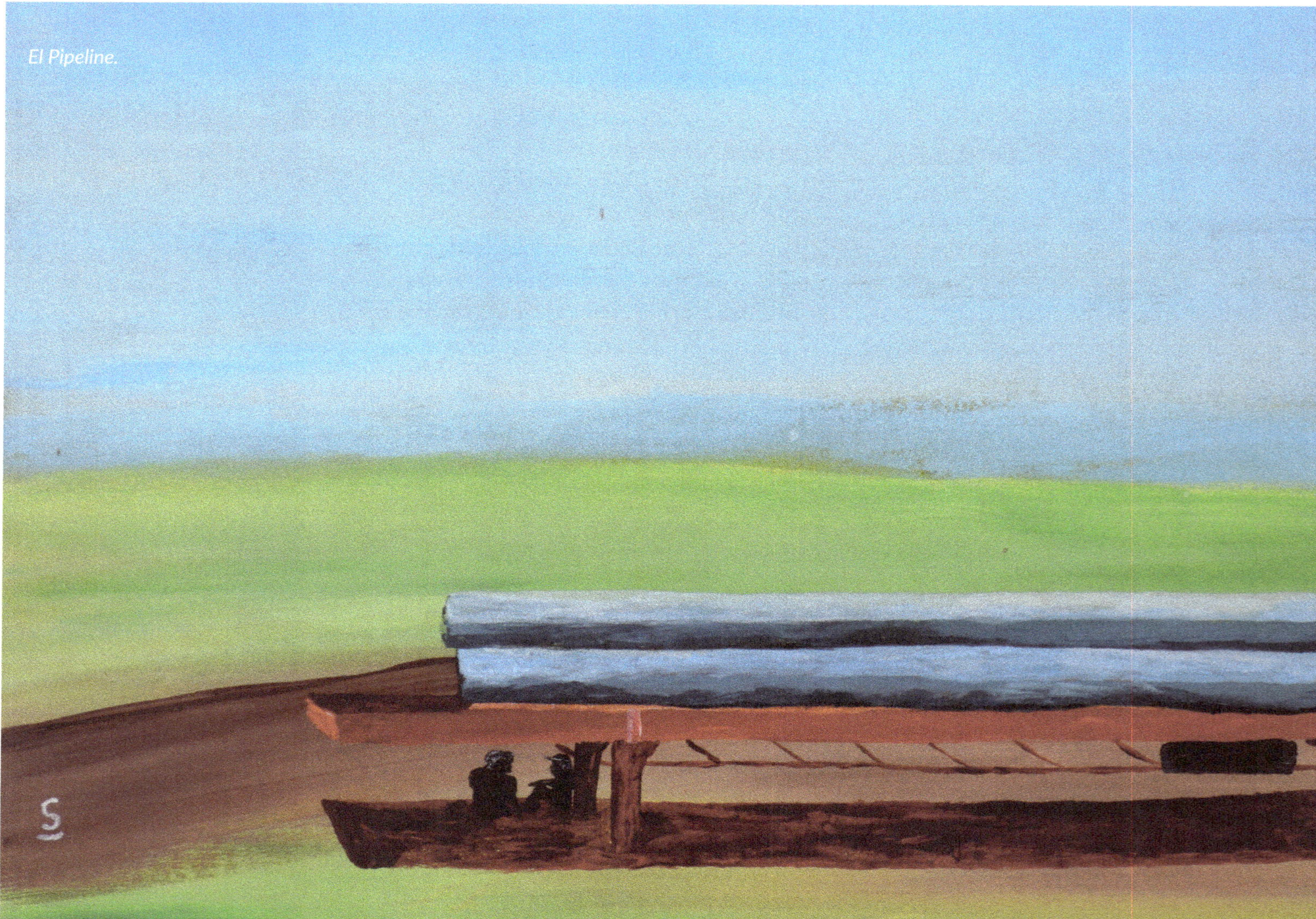
El Pipeline.

our lunch and sought refuge from the blistering sun under the trailer of an 18-wheeler. Dad heated the lunch with a propane torch and washed it down with the *café* mom sent. Mom's *taquitos* were delicious. After eating, *Papi* rolled a Bugler cigarette, smoked it, and then stretched out and took a short nap. Lunch was only thirty minutes, and he quickly got up and ordered everyone back to their work stations. The afternoon went much the same way as the morning.

At day's end, we headed back to where we were staying for the night. *Papi* and I had the last of my mom's *taquitos*. My brothers were "on their own." Most of the crew slept either in the motel rooms or behind the motel in trailers. *Papi*, my brothers, a guy I had never met before, and I slept in the same trailer house behind, but a part of the same motel.

The following morning everyone got up and met at the same convenience store. Dad bought stuff to eat and drink for breakfast. He also bought a couple of sodas and some canned food and crackers. I especially missed *Mami* then. We headed to the job-site, and they quickly started working.

At this time, the owner of the pipeline company showed up and I overheard my dad ask him if he could give me a ride home since he lived near us. He agreed, but before he did he asked me if I wanted to work. I said yes. Then he asked me how much an hour I charged. I gave him a figure that was about what my brothers were making. He did not agree to that, and I was on my way home that evening. I did not want to go home and told *Papi*, but he said I was too expensive, and was eating too much. I was, but I do not think that was the reason. I think he sent me home because I was too young and *Papi*, aside from overseeing the work crew and job-site, had to work at being a dad—always watching over me. I guess I was still too young to work in a place like "*el* pipeline". S

El tortillero (the tortilla maker)

In the 1970s stores did not sell flour tortillas and, like most Tejano families, our family had tortillas for every meal.

Mami called "*Mijito, ven hacer las tortillas. Los comales ya se están calentando.* Son, come and make the tortillas. The skillets are heating up.)"

Mami had cooked *arroz con pollo* (chicken and rice) for dinner, and it was my turn to learn how to make tortillas. Like most Tejano mothers she taught all of her sons and daughters how to make tortillas from scratch. In the 1970s stores did not sell flour tortillas and, like most Tejano families, our family had tortillas for every meal.

The recipe and the technique of how to make tortillas will remain forever etched in my memory.

1. *Llena una bandeja con harina y comienza a calentar una poca de agua.* (Fill a large pan with flour and start warming some water in a pan.)
2. *Ahora échale una poquita de espauda y sal a la harina.* (To the flour, add some baking powder and salt.)
3. *Échale otra poquita de sal.* (Add a little more salt.)
4. *Y ya cállate por que ya comenzó la novela.* (And now be quiet because my soap opera is back on.)
5. *OK. Ahora agarra una poquita de manteca y quiébrala en la harina.* (Now get a little more lard and mix it into the flour.)

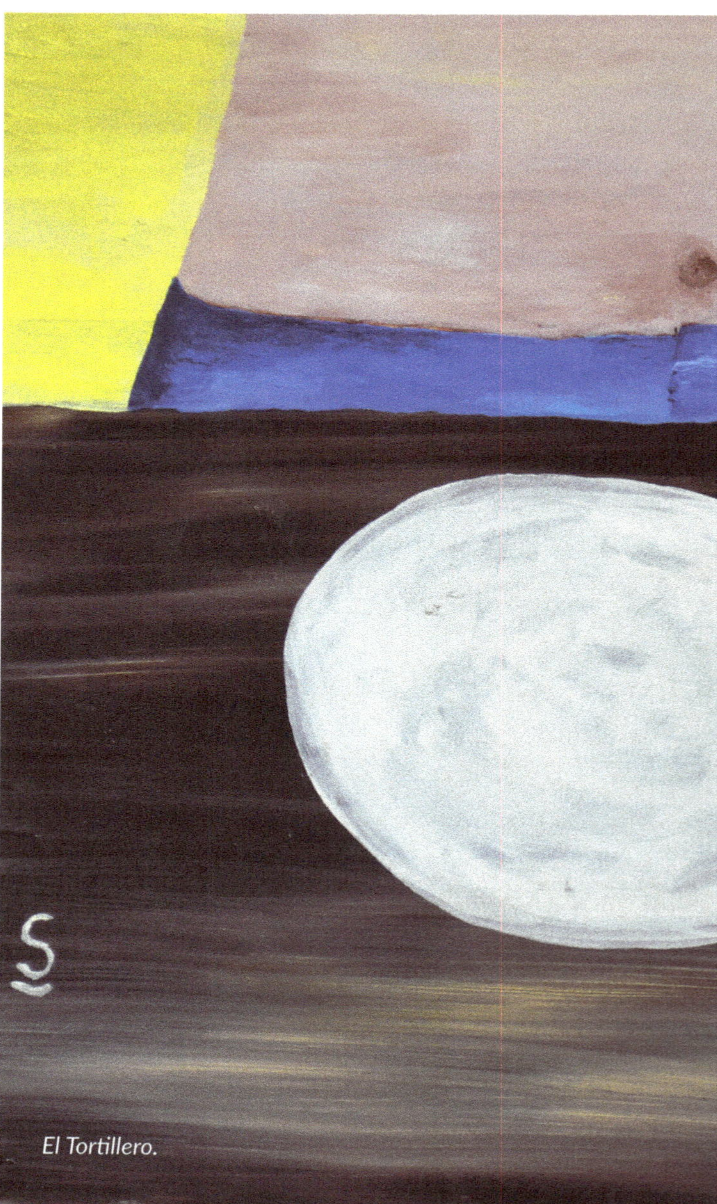

El Tortillero.

6. *Ahora agarra agua tibia y échasela a la harina y haz la masa.* (Now get some tepid water and add to the flour to make the dough.)

7. *Deja que la masa se siente por cinco minutos y después haz los testales.* (Let the dough sit for about five minutes and make balls of dough.)

8. *Ahora extiende los testales con el palote y que queden redonditos, luego pon la tortilla en el comal y espera a que se esponje antes de voltearla.* (Then you flatten the dough balls with a rolling pin until they are round, and then place the tortilla in the comal and wait for it to sponge up before flipping it to the other side.)

9. *Repite lo mismo por dos o tres veces más, hasta que la tortilla tenga manchitas cafés por los dos lados.* (Repeat this step two or three times until the tortilla has brown spots on both sides.)

The aroma of cooking tortillas quickly spread throughout the house. Since most households did not have air conditioning, windows were opened and the aroma quickly spread throughout the colonia. The aroma of cooking tortillas is very recognizable and intoxicating, and quickly stops people in their tracks and lures them to its source. What joy for those identifying that place as their own home! §

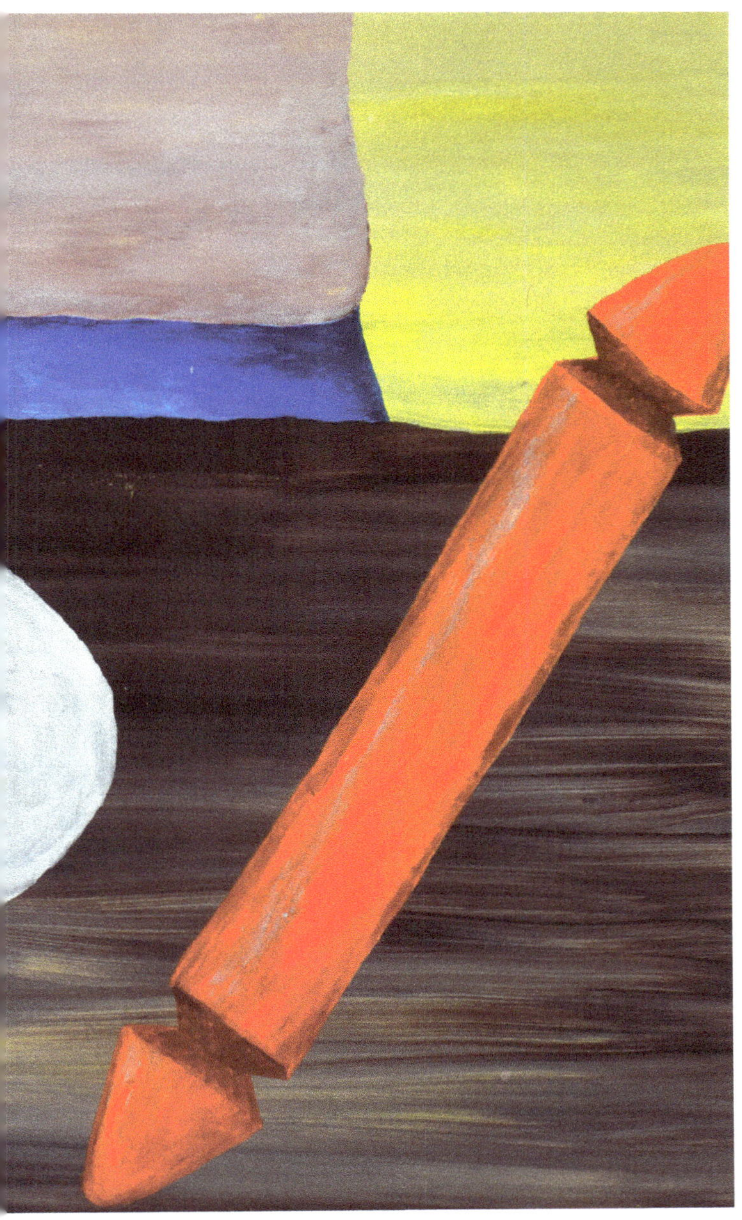

Sandia barata
(Cheap Watermelon)

Somehow *Papi* knew when the *sandia* were ripe in the fields and he took two of his teenage sons to pick them. All of his boys picked watermelons before leaving the Soto household. Through the years, we went to Falfurrias, Riviera, Sandia, and Stockdale. Since Sandia was closest to home, we went there the most.

Before leaving in early morning, we cleaned the bed of the pickup and put some *faldones* (sideboards) on both sides of the pickup so we could haul plenty of watermelons. As soon as we got to the farmer's house, he directed us to the field that needed picking. We filled the pickup about halfway, and then we stopped and *Papi* sliced a *sandia* and we ate as much as we could, spitting out the seeds.

There is nothing like eating hot watermelon on a warm sunny day. I thought Papi was being nice giving us a snack for our hard work, but it was more of a tasting exercise. Since sweet watermelons are more marketable he needed to make sure that the *sandia* was sweet. We were his tasters.

We then finished loading the watermelons, Papi and the farmer estimated how many watermelons were in the bed of the pickup, and

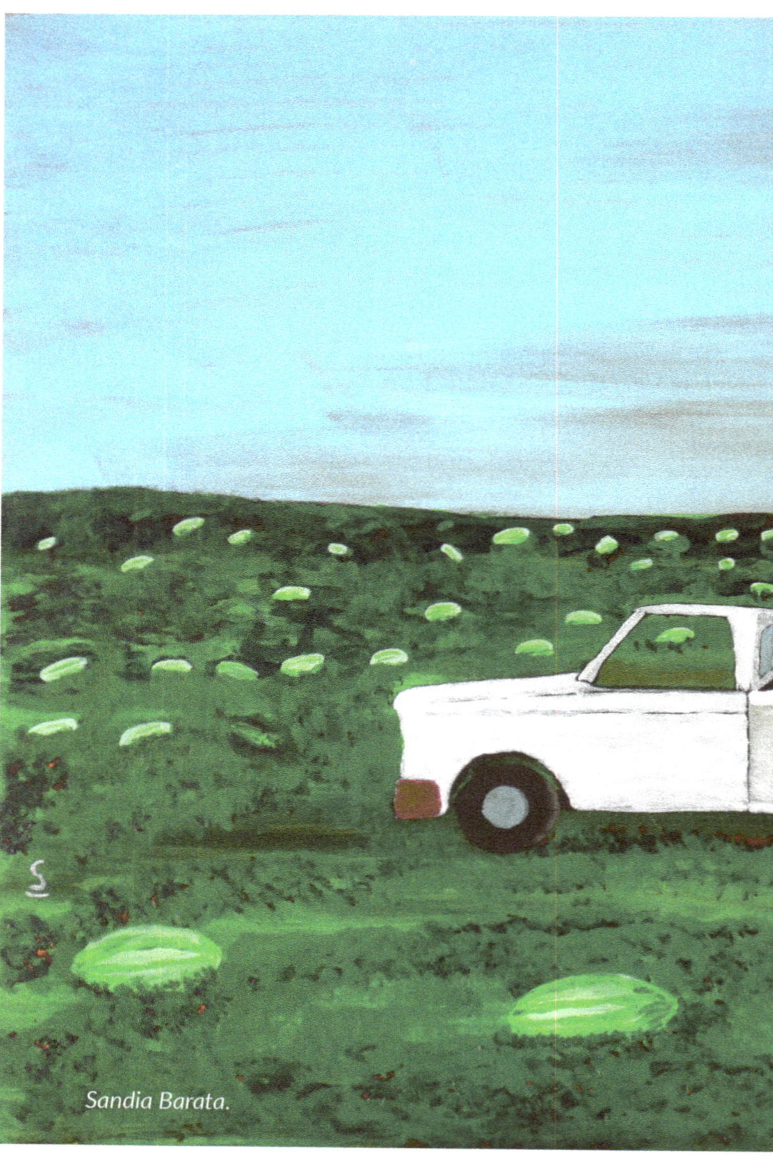

Sandia Barata.

the farmer set his price. My dad usually responded by saying, "¡a chingau!" (Damn!), and the farmer dropped the price a little. They shook on the deal and Papi paid him.

When we got back home to Edroy, *Papi* assigned one of the older brothers or sisters to drive the pickup around town honking the horn, while the rest of us sat in the bed of the pickup yelling out our sales pitch "*sandia barata, sandia barata, están bien dulce, están garantizadas* (cheap watermelon, cheap watermelon, very sweet, guaranteed)." The pickup stopped frequently and we knocked on doors to ask if they wanted *sandia barata*. Sometimes this was frightening since some folks had mean dogs.

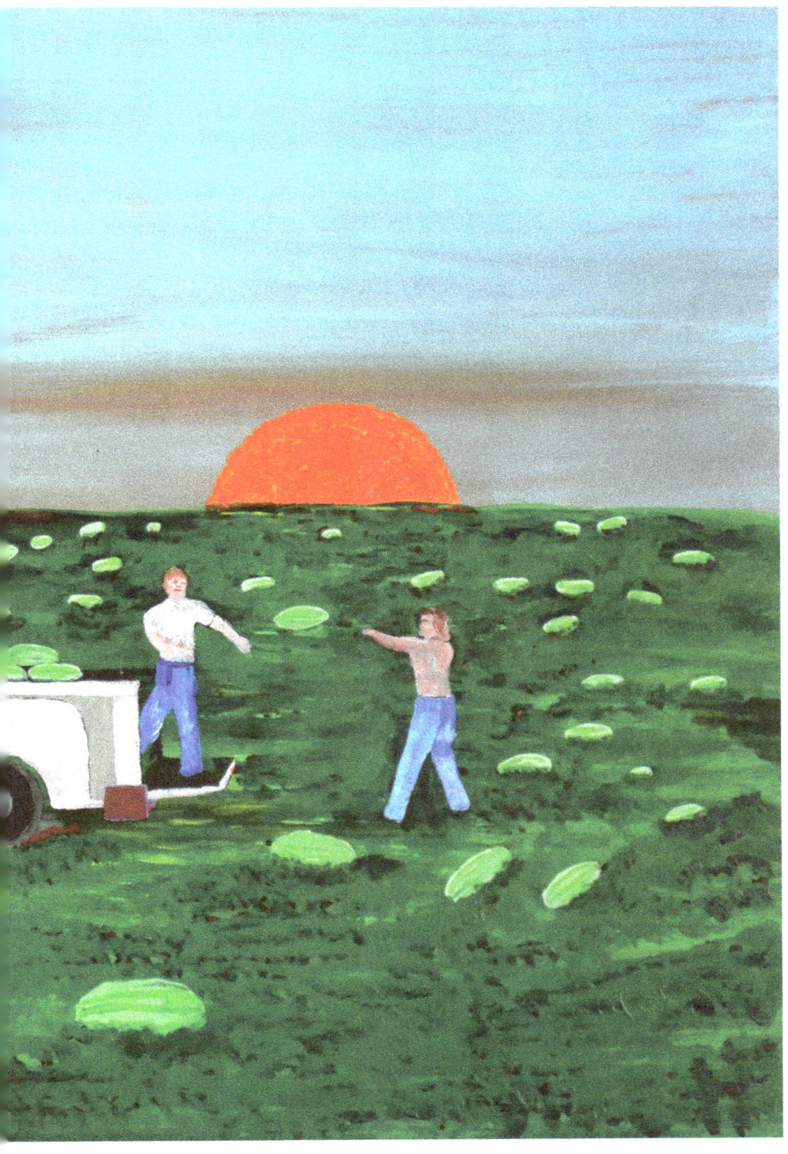

The watermelons not sold that day were stored on our porch. We formed a human chain and tossed the watermelons to the next person in line. Catching the watermelons could be hard, especially when a younger sibling was being thrown a 30-pound watermelon from a physically mature, but mentally immature older sibling.

The stored watermelons were sold to walk-in customers and the family ate some as snacks for weeks. The children, who did all the work, did not get to keep any of the money from the *sandia* sales.

El bofe (The lung)

My cousin, Esperanza recalls calling out, "*Buela, buela, ahi viene el bofe! Ahi viene el bofe!* (Grandma, grandma there comes the lung!) *Páralo mijita! Páralo!* (Stop him little one, stop him.)"

In the 1950s, Señor Benavidez worked at a large cattle ranch, which was later converted to a cattle feedlot. When a cow accidentally died, the workers—including *Señor Benavidez*—butchered it and were allowed to take the offal home. These innards, such as the heart, lungs, liver, lungs, tripe, etc. were seen by slaughtering houses as worthless and were often thrown out with the garbage.

Señor Benavidez knew that Tejanos were not prone to waste edible food, so he loaded the offal in a wheelbarrow and hauled it, along with a cloud of hungry flies, about half a mile to Edroy. At first he gave it away, but he quickly realized that some of those items were in demand and could fetch a modest price so he began to sell every part of the offal.

Esperanza remembers this well. She recalls helping *Abuelita* make *picadillo de bofe* (lung hash). The *bofe* was boiled for a couple of hours and then strained and diced to fairly small pieces. Onion, garlic, black pepper, salt, comino, and garlic were sautéed in a pan. A couple of diced tomatoes were added later. The ingredients were cooked to make fairly light tomato based gravy. *Abuela* served this enticing entrée with *frijolitos* and gave those partaking in the dish a choice of homemade corn or flour tortillas.

Esperanza still remembers the taste of the picadillo saying, "*estaba bien sabroso* (it was delicious)," as she rolled her eyes and smiled. (*Bofe* is no longer eaten in the United States, as the USDA prohibits the use of livestock lungs as human food. It is still eaten in other parts of the world). **S**

> *Señor Benavidez knew that Tejanos were not prone to waste edible food, so he loaded the offal in a wheelbarrow and hauled it, followed by a cloud of hungry flies...*

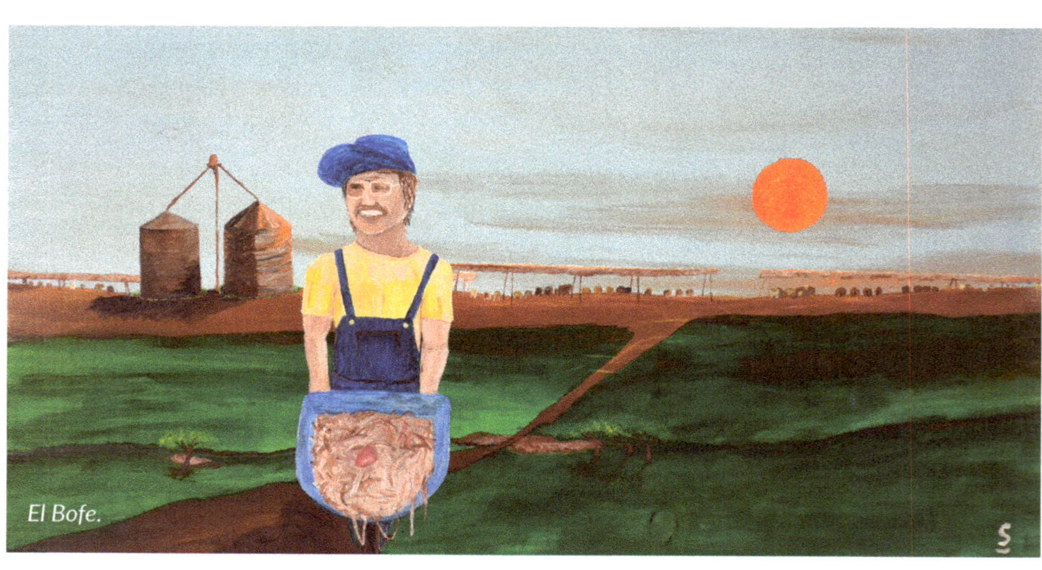
El Bofe.

Pelón pelucas (hairless wigs)

The school year was about to begin and I overheard *Papi* asking *Mami*, "*Carranzina, dónde están las clipas*" (Carranzina, where are the hair clippers). *Mami* found them with no problem. What was difficult to find were all the boys that were hiding in the house and throughout the neighborhood? There were boys hiding in closets and under beds. Some even ran away from home.

It was haircut day in Edroy and my dad was also the neighborhood barber, although he had no formal training. Each one tried to tell him how they wanted their hair cut, but he did not listen. He started cutting his sons' hair first, and then other fathers drove to our house asking *Papi* "how much?" He yelled to them, "*Cincuenta centavos por uno o tres por un peso* (Fifty cents for one haircut or three for a dollar)."

One by one, each boy reluctantly and sometimes forcefully sat on that dreaded chair. If the boy was not already crying as he sat on the chair, he would soon be as *Papi* turned on the clippers and the ominous buzz became louder and louder as it neared the ears.

It was over in two or three minutes, after which each boy went into hiding once again. The name-calling began immediately; "*pelón pelucas*".

One by one, each boy reluctantly and some-times force-fully sat on that dreaded chair. If the boy was not already crying as he sat on the chair, he would soon be as *Papi* turned on the clippers...

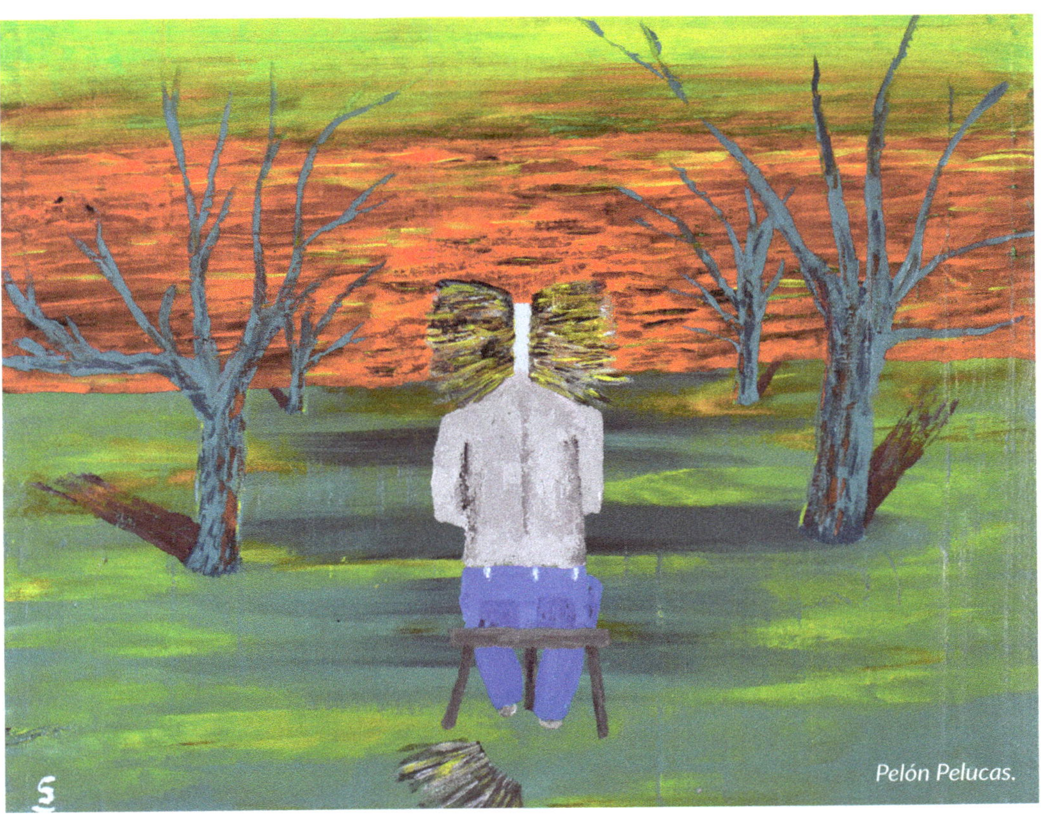

Pelón Pelucas.

Rosario

As any Tejano from a big family knows, the children sometimes had to share beds. I was two-years-old and my first sleeping mate was my sister Rosario, whom we called "Rosy". At the time, Rosy was in high school and the oldest sister still living at home. I am not sure who made this sleeping arrangement, *Mami* or Rosy, but I do remember that I was supposed to take care of Rosy and make sure she was safe at night, away from the *cucuys* (goblins).

Rosy was the best lullaby singer ever, and she knew lots of songs. She had a pretty voice and even had the ability to change her voice to a deep baritone. It was so cool!

One day in 1973, Rosy did not come home from school. My mother sent my oldest brother Juan to go look for her. Juan went to Rosy's boyfriend Freddy's house. They were not there. He went to Freddy's friend's house, Manuel, and asked him where they were. He did not know.

Rosy was pregnant and scared and had gone to church after school. Freddy had borrowed his friend Manuel's 1964 pale yellow Ford Falcon. They were going to elope.

I had never seen my mother so upset as she was when she heard the news. She was so mad, it shook the whole house.

I thought it was my fault. When Rosy and Freddy came back, my mom told her, "*Ya vete de aquí. Tú pa' mí ya estás muerta* (Get out of here. You are already dead to me)." My dad was more understanding

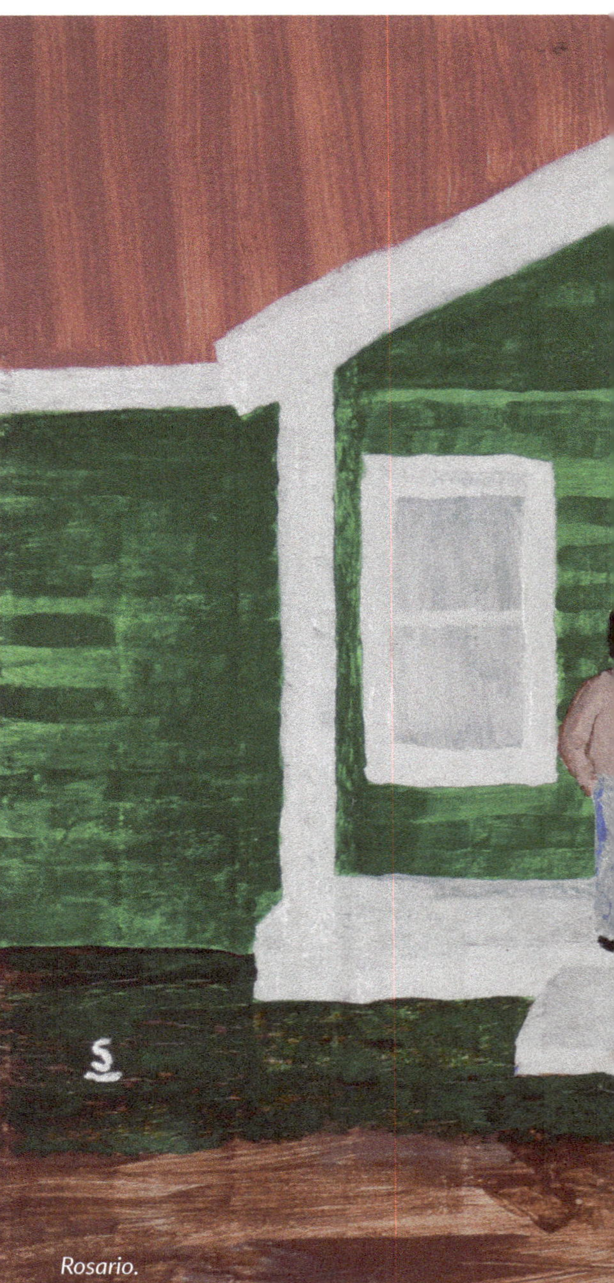

Rosario.

and told my mom, "*ya apasíguate*" (calm down).

After several weeks, my mom settled down, and as Rosy and Freddy left my mom and my *Abuelita* prayed a *rosario* to bless them in their new life. Abel was born sometime later, and they had four additional kids.

The whole family still enjoys listening to Freddy's beautiful baritone voice. 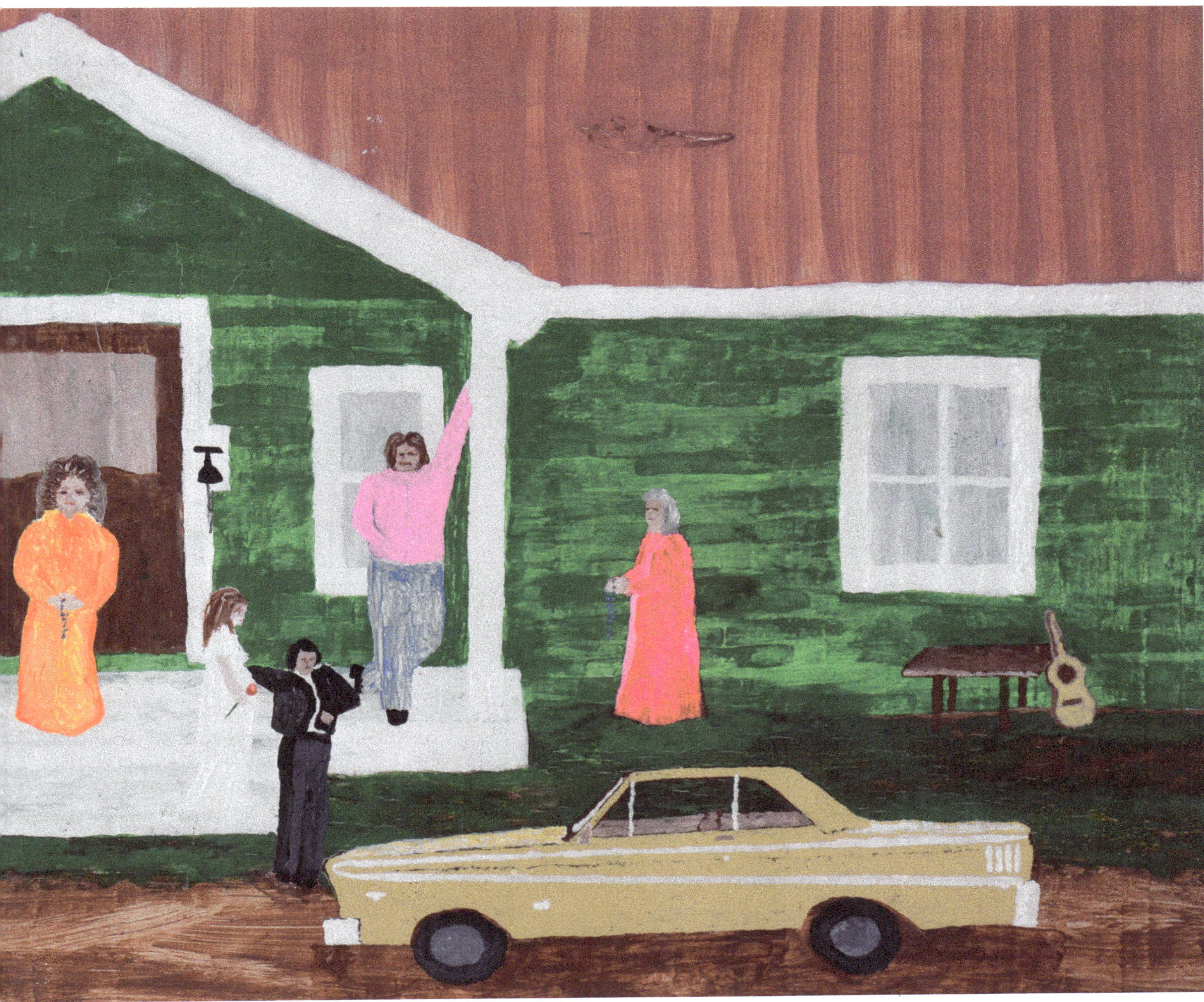

Oorah

Papi was out of town again working *"en el* pipeline". *Mami* had already made *frijolitos* and eggs for breakfast, with homemade tortillas too. She had everyone ready to catch the bus. She had help now. My brother Mandito, Cpl. Amando C. Soto, had served two years in the United States Marine Corp and had temporarily moved back in with us.

The Soto household was different. I am not talking about the minor changes in sleeping arrangements. Oorahs resonated throughout the house and yard. OORAH!!!!!

Aside from Mandito, it was a typical school morning, at least as an eight-year-old boy remembers it. The outhouse was a busy place, and the boys brushed their teeth outside next to the faucet.

Mandito received some training in plumbing from the Marines, and had the idea that with our help we could install an indoor toilet. Oorah! *Papi* was against the toilet idea because he said it would be too much of a burden on a septic tank, but the marine got his way.

I still remember us crawling under the house and cutting and fitting the pipes for the toilet. The sound of oorahs echoed even louder then. It was so unbearable and intimidating that even the pipes, trembling with fear, surrendered and the plumbing was quickly finished.

After several days of oorahs, the toilet was ready for inauguration.

Since we did not have a bathroom door, *Mami* sewed a nice curtain for privacy.

Mandito picked me to break it in. He told me to make sure the toilet was working properly that it

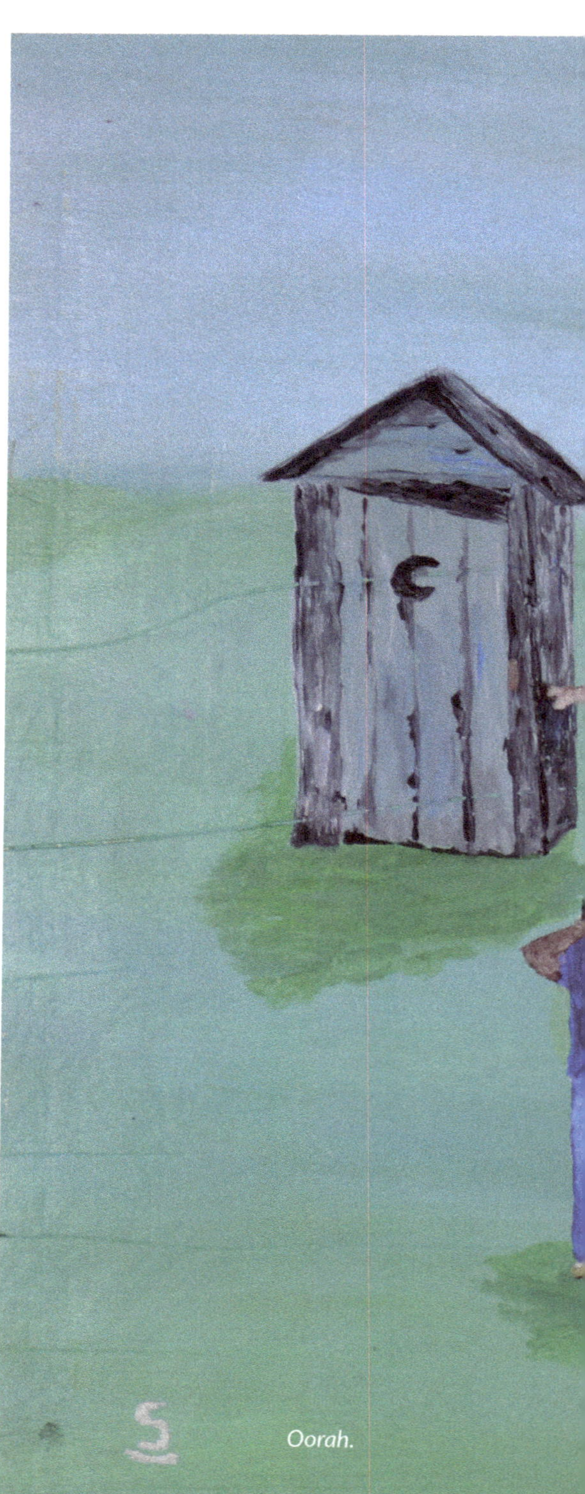

Oorah.

had to be flushed with *poopoo* in it. He ordered me to go use it. I told him, "*no tengo ganas* (I do not need to go)." He was persistent. After a while, he finally convinced me to use the bathroom even though I really did not have to. I tried and tried. While sitting on the toilet, at the height of concentration, ready to expel what little was in my bowels, the curtain flew open and Mandito took my picture. §

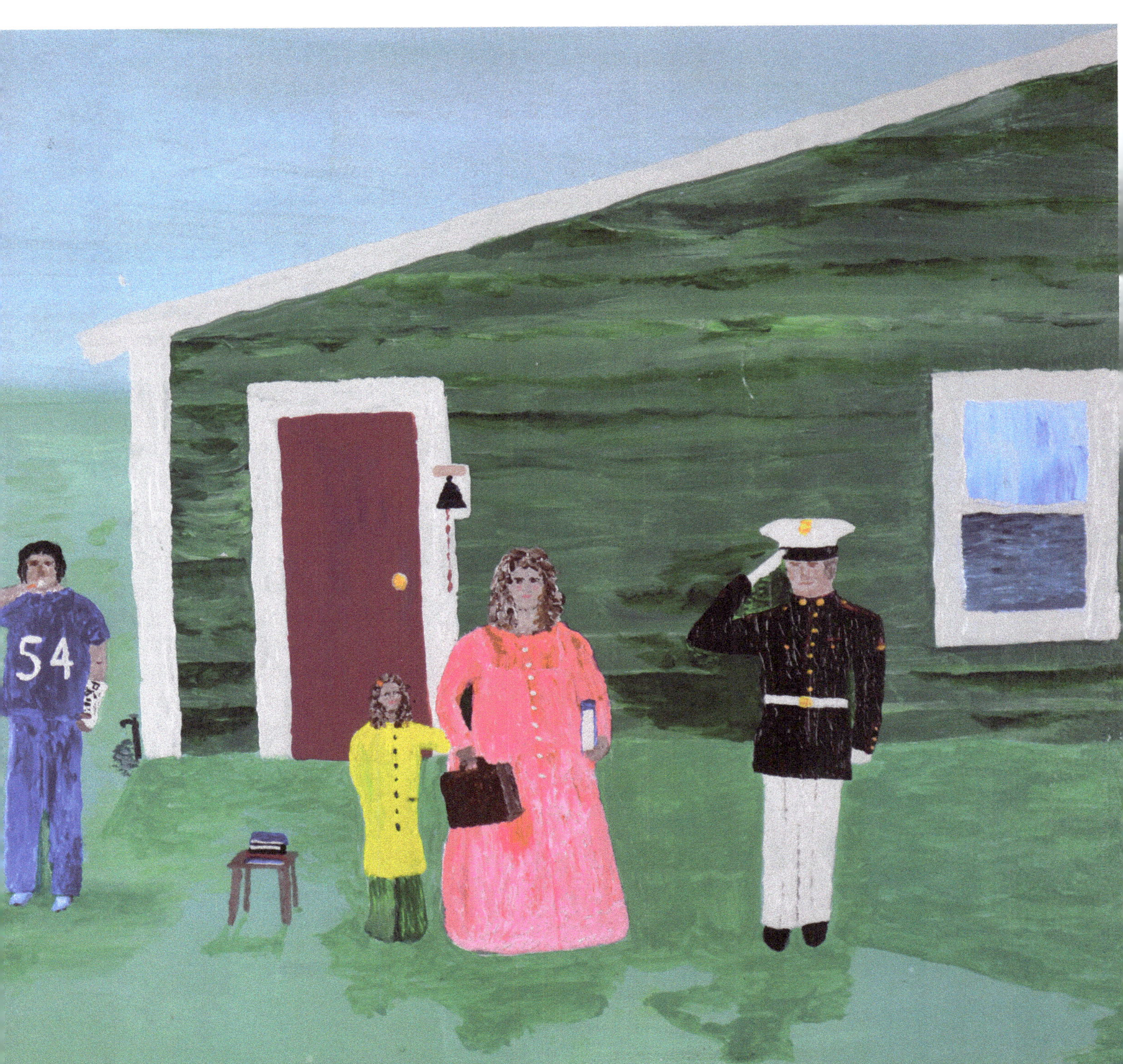

Hitchhiking

Edroy never had permanent school. Children went to school in Odem, six miles away. In the 1950s – 1990s, two or three buses were sent to Edroy to pick up students at about seven in the morning and drop them off at about four in the afternoon. No buses were available to transport students if they had an extracurricular activity after school. They relied on their parents to pick them up after a practice or an event.

Although almost everyone had work, most households were economically challenged. Very few families could afford the extra cost of picking up their kids from extracurricular activities. I remember *Papi* saying, "*si quieres jugar pelota busca en que ir y vale más que no te lastimes* (If you want to play ball you got to find your own way home and you better not get hurt)."

Most boys started hitchhiking from Odem to Edroy in the second grade when they were eligible to play little league baseball, and the hitchhiking continued until their last sporting event, which was usually at the end of their senior year. Girls usually were not allowed to hitchhike home, so they had minimal involvement in extracurricular activities.

On any given evening there was a steady stream of up 10-12 boys walking and waiting at the hitchhiking pickup spot at the outskirts of Odem. One of the boys signaled with his thumb, the universal hitchhiking sign, and it took from five minutes to an hour to get picked up.

There are always risks when hitchhiking, but I never heard of anyone having bad experiences attributed to hitchhiking. Normally, local folks on the way home from work picked us up. Occasionally, strangers offered us rides and that was always a little scary.

If a car stopped, two or three of us jumped in and the rest waited for the next car. If it was a pickup, we all jumped in the back. This was especially challenging when it was very cold. The weather was mostly tolerable during football and baseball seasons since they took place in the spring, summer, and fall. I did not play basketball; it was cold!

On a few occasions we got picked up by some misguided young adults. They were coming home from work. They drove with the windows rolled up and got stoned in the car, with us in it! As soon as we got in the car, they said, "We're gonna have a smoke out", and then laughed and laughed. Most young people were exposed to marijuana at a very early age. Some smoked and some did not.

At times, some good natured people that were not going to Edroy picked us up and took us home. One of my best friends lived about a mile from Odem on the main road to Edroy. They were farmers, and their cars usually had the hitchhiking sign, "Gig 'em Aggies", on the back windshield. My friend had two older, college age sisters that were two of the most beautiful girls in Odem. Sometimes they picked me up and took me home. I was never as quiet as I was when in their cars. §

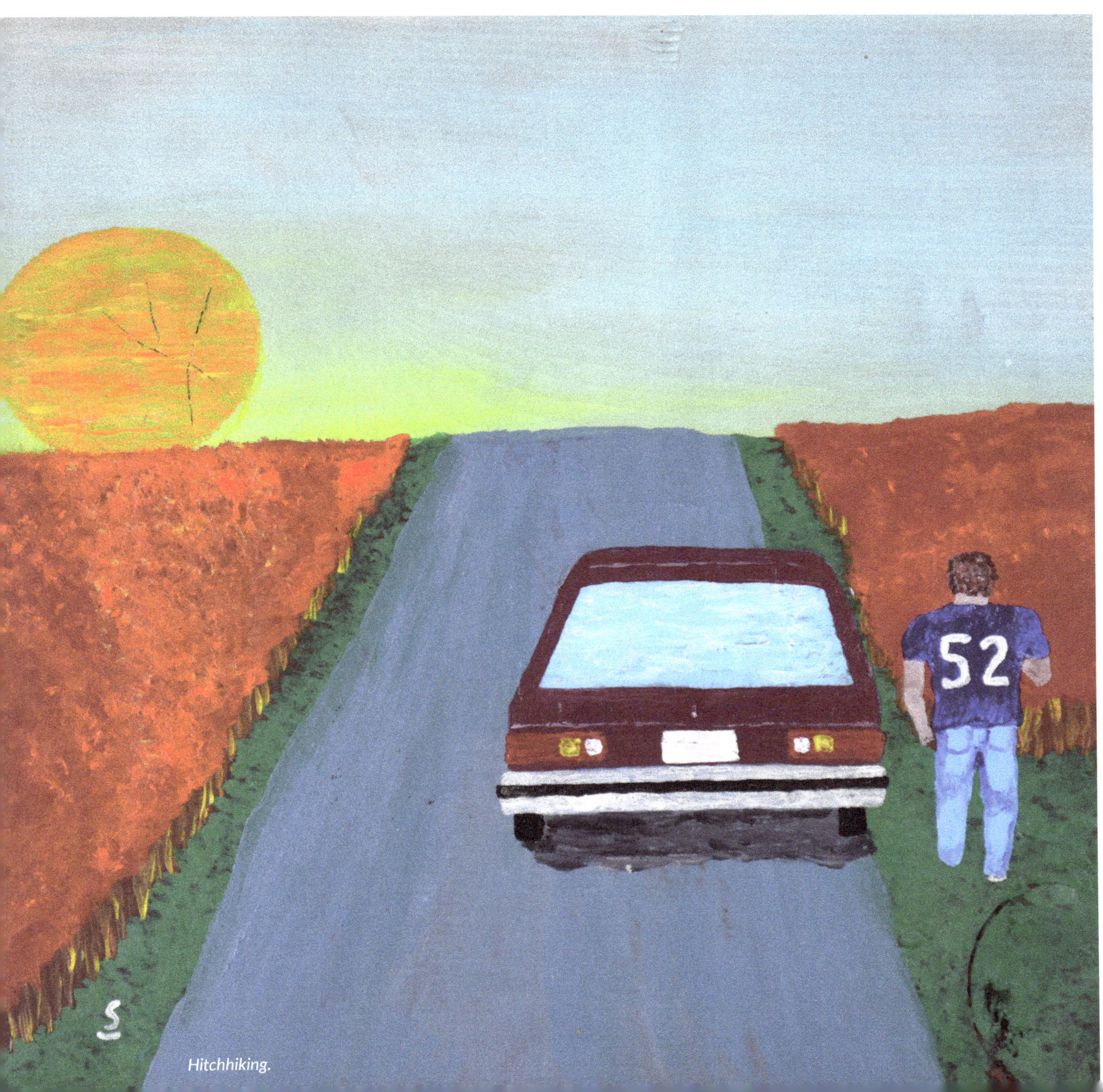

Hitchhiking.

El molino (the mill)

It was summer, and I was fifteen years old. I usually worked with *Papi* in the summers, but he was getting older and was slowing down. He did not have much work. I knew, like most Tejano young men, I was expected to buy school clothes for the year and have some money for miscellaneous activities throughout the year. I also wanted to save money for college.

Early one morning, I applied for work at the local grain elevator, *el molino*. At the end of the day, Mr. Benavidez who was the foreman went to my house and told me to punch in at seven the next morning.

In South Texas farmers plant sorghum. By late June and early July it turns a beautiful vermilion and is ready to harvest. In the 1980s, sorghum was harvested

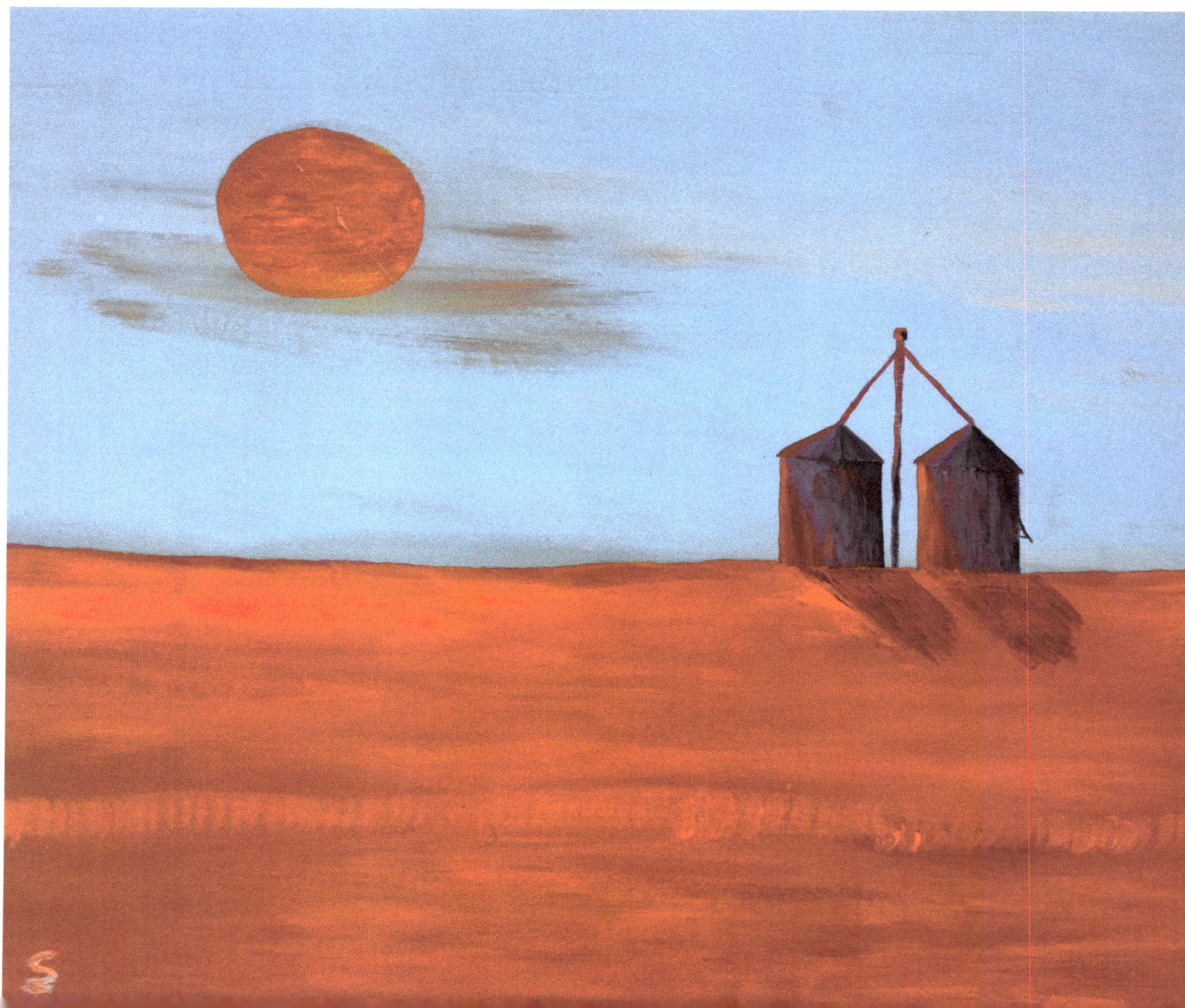

using specialized tractors that cut the grain from the rest of the plant. The grain was loaded onto big trucks or trailers and then hauled to a grain elevator. At the elevator, the grain was weighed, tested, and dumped into a pit, from where the grain elevator picked it up and dumped it into pipes for distribution into various grain storage tanks (bins) or grain houses.

The grain is stored in these facilities until it is sold.

In preparation for the harvest, the tanks and houses had to be cleaned. One of my duties was to help clean them, which involved shoveling all day. We worked about forty-five hours a week in preparation for the harvest. In our area, harvest started around the last week of June or the first week of July.

My other responsibilities were to unload the grain trucks, weigh, and sample the grain. When handled, grain releases clouds of dust that pose a hazard when inhaled. It is also very itchy and flammable. The workers, including myself, had to take precaution and wore a dust mask to keep from inhaling the dust. Usually, we wore the mask all day. If the skin was directly exposed to the dust it caused an intense itching that lasted for days. There are many anecdotal remedies for the itching but none worked on me.

When working with grain dust all day, it also cakes up in your eyes. I woke up one morning with both my eyes sealed shut and was only able to open them after I rinsed warm water over them. Nothing was worn to protect the eyes.

I wanted more work and I got it. When harvesting was well underway we worked every day from seven in the morning to when the last truck was unloaded for the day, usually about nine or eleven at

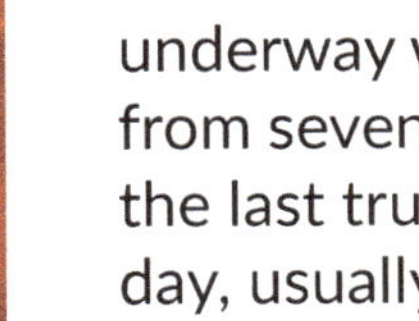

Vermilion Summer.

night. Working ninety to 105 hours a week was common during peak harvest. The most I ever worked in one week was ninety-six hours. Multiply that by the minimum wage at the time of $3.35/hour, and time and a half after forty hours, and my pay for that week was about $400.

I worked at the grain elevator until the harvest was over and football practice started in mid-August.

The following year I was not quite sure whether I was going to work the elevator again that summer. On the last day of the school year, Mr. Benavidez stopped me and told me to go punch in the next day at the usual time. I worked the rest of my high school summers there and two additional summers while in college.

The grain elevator employed many permanent and seasonal workers. It also employed many high school and college students. It was exhausting, filthy, and risky work, but it did provide other students and me with a much needed source of income. §

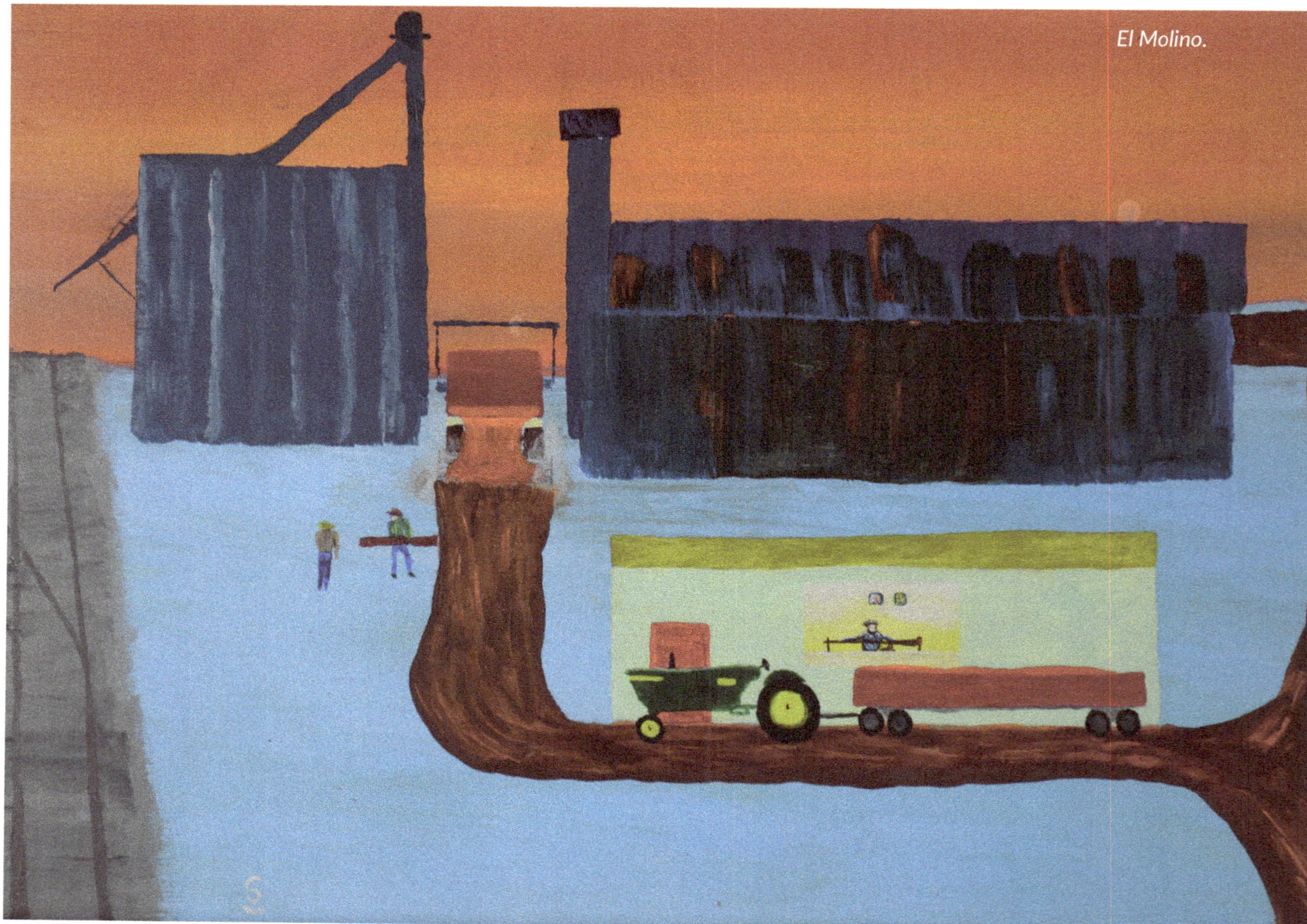

El Molino.

Grit

Southouth Texas has a long history of ethnic tension between Tejanos and Anglos. In the 1960s, *Papi*, my oldest brother Juan, and another teenager from Edroy, were working *en el* pipeline a few towns north of Edroy. Before work, they stopped for breakfast at a local restaurant. After sitting at a table and being overlooked by staff several times, *Papi* told Juan, "*A mí se me hace que no nos van a servir* (I believe they are not going to serve us)." They left.

Tejanos experiencing blatant discrimination was a common occurrence in the 1960s. On another occasion, my sister Balbina was a member of the high school band that was going out of town for a football game. They stopped to eat at a restaurant in a neighboring town, and the management refused service to the Tejano members, despite already sitting at a table. They eventually were served, but only after they heard pleas from the adult sponsor of the trip.

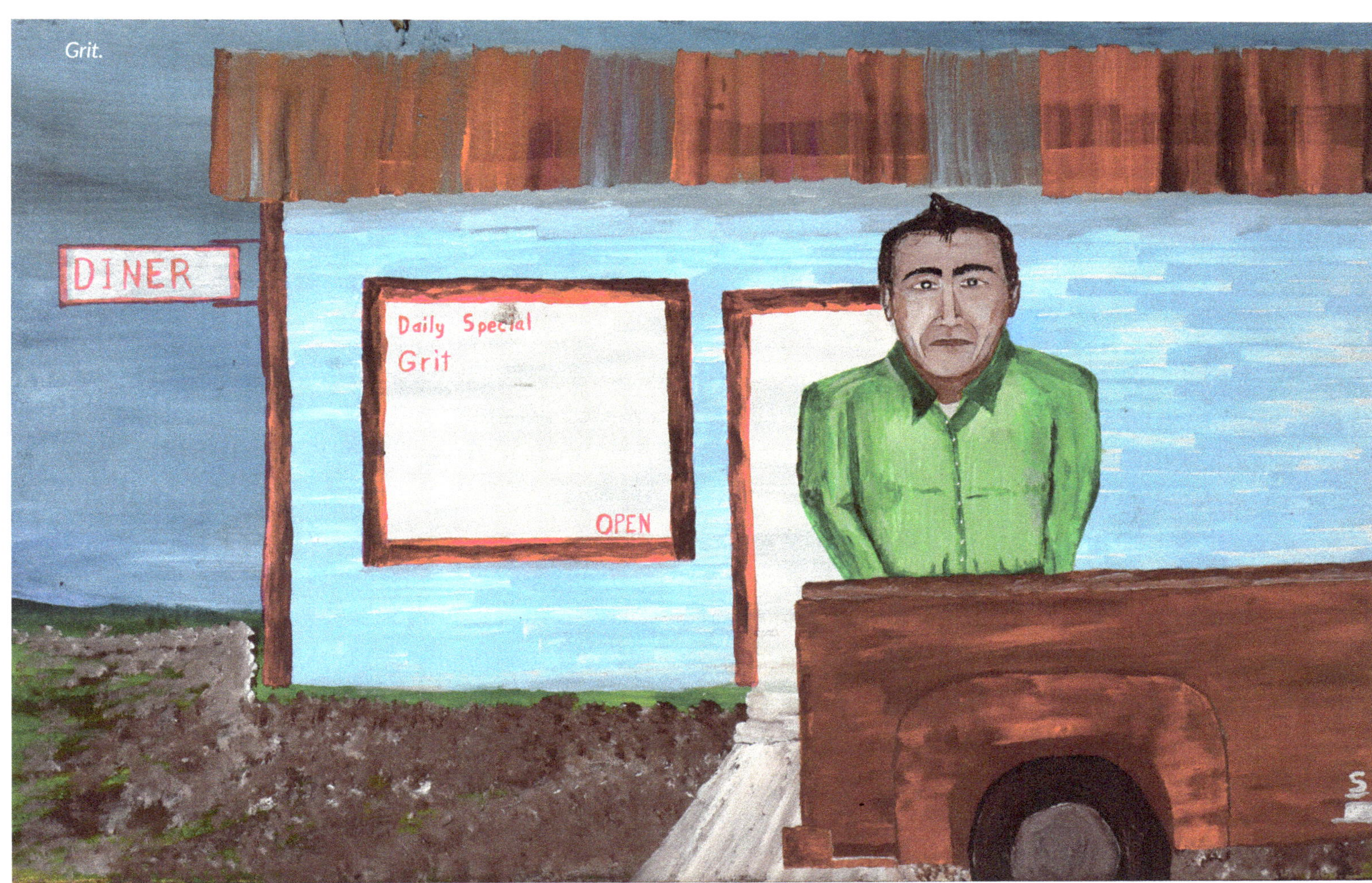

La Toronja y La Marrana (The Grapefruit and The Sow)

As mentioned earlier, in the 1950s and through the early 1970s, several families from Edroy went a *la pizca*. They were migrant workers and helped harvest most types of agricultural products throughout the United States, including potatoes in Idaho, cotton in Texas, and citrus in Florida.

Two of the boys growing up at the time of these migrations were my cousin, Richard "Riche" Soto and my oldest brother, Juan. They were best friends and loved

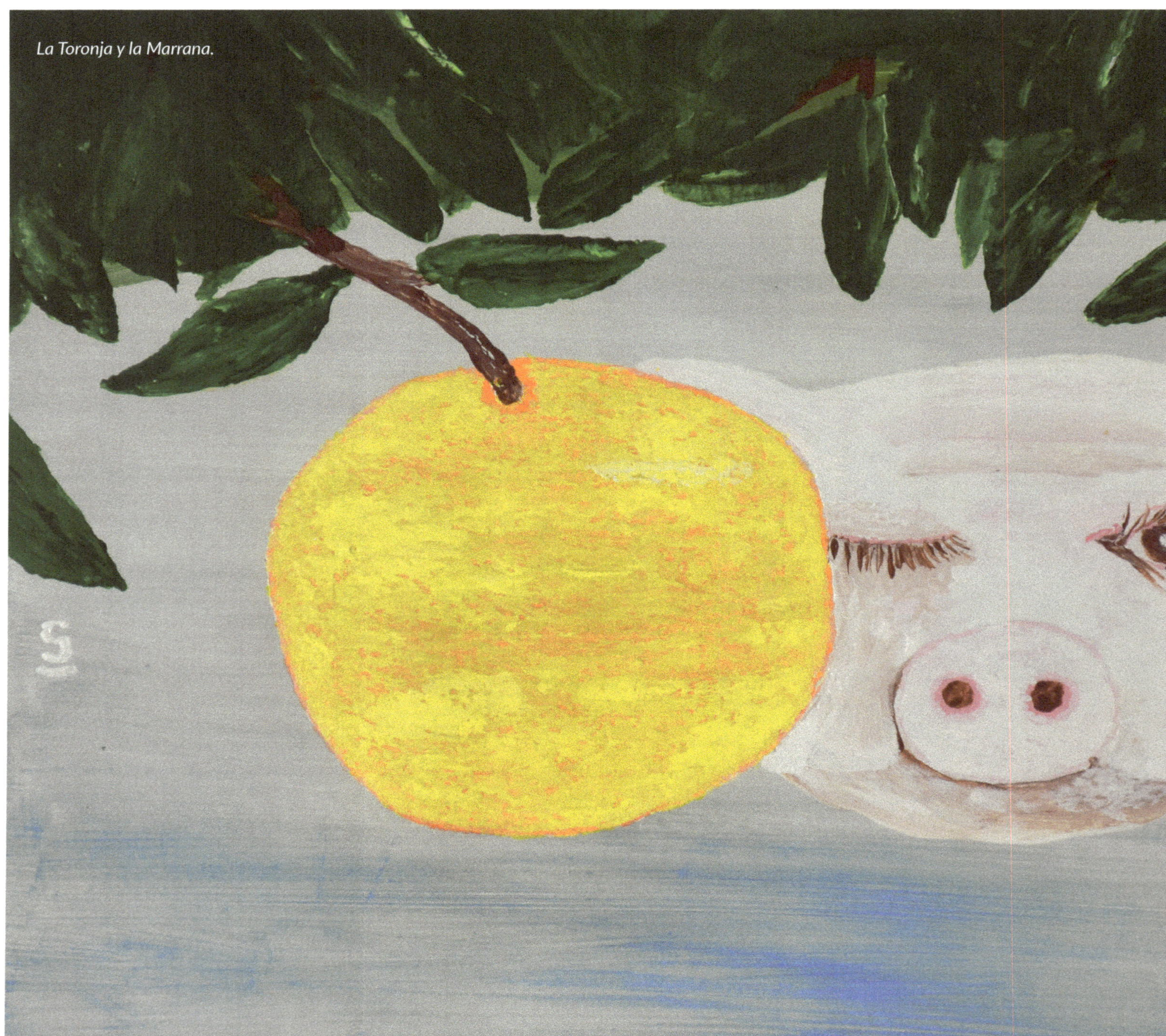

La Toronja y la Marrana.

each other deeply, but working was the last thing on their minds. They were lackadaisical and better known for their rambunctious and mischievous ways. In fact, they were best known for stealing taquitos from the workers while they were out picking. As a result, both boys became *gorditos* (fatties) and it was during this time that they earned their nicknames.

Riche was called *La Toronja*, and my brother was *Juana La Marrana*. Just about every male in town— and in South Texas for that matter—had a nickname. In our town, my father usually assigned nicknames. In our family, there was: *La Teta* (the baby bottle) because he sucked his thumb, *El Zorrillo* (The Skunk) because he wet the bed, *La Masa* (The Dough) because he was slightly overweight, *El Dodge* (The Dodge) because *Papi* had to sell a black pickup to pay the doctor to deliver him and was also born dark complected, *El Coyote* (The Coyote) a name usually given to the baby of the family. Our neighbors were *La Espira* (The Spider), *La Máscara* (The Mask), *El Tacuache* (The Possum), and *La Liebre* (The Jackrabbit). Other notable nicknames in Edroy were: *El Mofle* (The Muffler), *El Moco* (The Booger), *La Rata* (The Rat) and *La Rata's* son *La Ratita (The Little Rat)*.

Tejanos possess a variety of distinct physical traits that are found in their Native American and European ancestors. These traits were the basis of some of the nicknames assigned to some individuals, *El Güero* (The Light Skinned One), *El Prieto* (The Dark One), *El Indio* (The Indian), *Kansas*, and *El Filipino* (The Philippine). ◪

El *azadón* (the hoe)

Papi gritó, "Esta medio pesado, agarren dos surcos pa' cada lado y vámonos (It's kind of heavy, get two rows to each side and let's go)." He was referring to the heavy amount of weeds that were growing among the cotton plants. He told each person of the crew to only hoe the weeds from two rows of cotton to each side. If there were not too many weeds among the plants each person covered four or even six rows to each side.

Throughout the mid to late 1900s, seeing Tejanos walk up and down South Texas *labores* (fields) was common. They were seasonally employed to hoe weeds in cotton fields, which was also referred to as el *desahijé* (the grubbing). *Papi* and *muchos otros hombres viejos* (many other older men) from Edroy were the foremen of this activity. Each foreman had a verbal agreement with the farmer to chop the weeds in their fields. The foreman then assembled a crew.

I remember both men and women from all age groups going to the house and asking *Papi* for work. He rarely denied anyone. He told each person to meet outside our house the next morning and to bring their own hoe and lunch. *Papi* supplied a jug of drinking water and transportation. The water was cooled with a block of ice, which my mom made by filling an empty gallon ice cream container with water and placing it in the freezer.

At seven in the morning, the crew assembled outside the house, the water jug and hoes were placed onto *Papi*'s pickup and the crew jumped in. Two of the older crew members sat with my dad in the cab and the rest of us, including some older ladies and gentlemen, rode on the bed.

After arriving at the field, my dad parked the pickup at the head rows. Each member made sure his hoe was sharpened and everyone put on their sombrero. Everyone knew to wear pants and a long sleeve shirt. We walked up and down the field hoeing weeds all day taking short breaks for water and sometimes a snack. Lunch was thirty minutes. These jobs lasted from a week to several weeks at the beginning of summer.

My first job in the *azadón* lasted only a short time. It was the summer of 1981 and I was about eleven-years-old. An older brother and I were working for *Papi*. That particular time, some of our neighbors went along, including *La Espida*, who was four years older than me. We were right next to each other walking the fields when one of us threw a dirt clot at the other. In retaliation, another dirt clot was thrown. *Papi* gave *La Espida* and me a ride back home. We were fired.

Throughout my life and all the jobs I have ever had, *Papi* was the only man that ever fired me, and he did that many, many times and not to just to me. He fired his other sons and anyone that worked for him. ◾

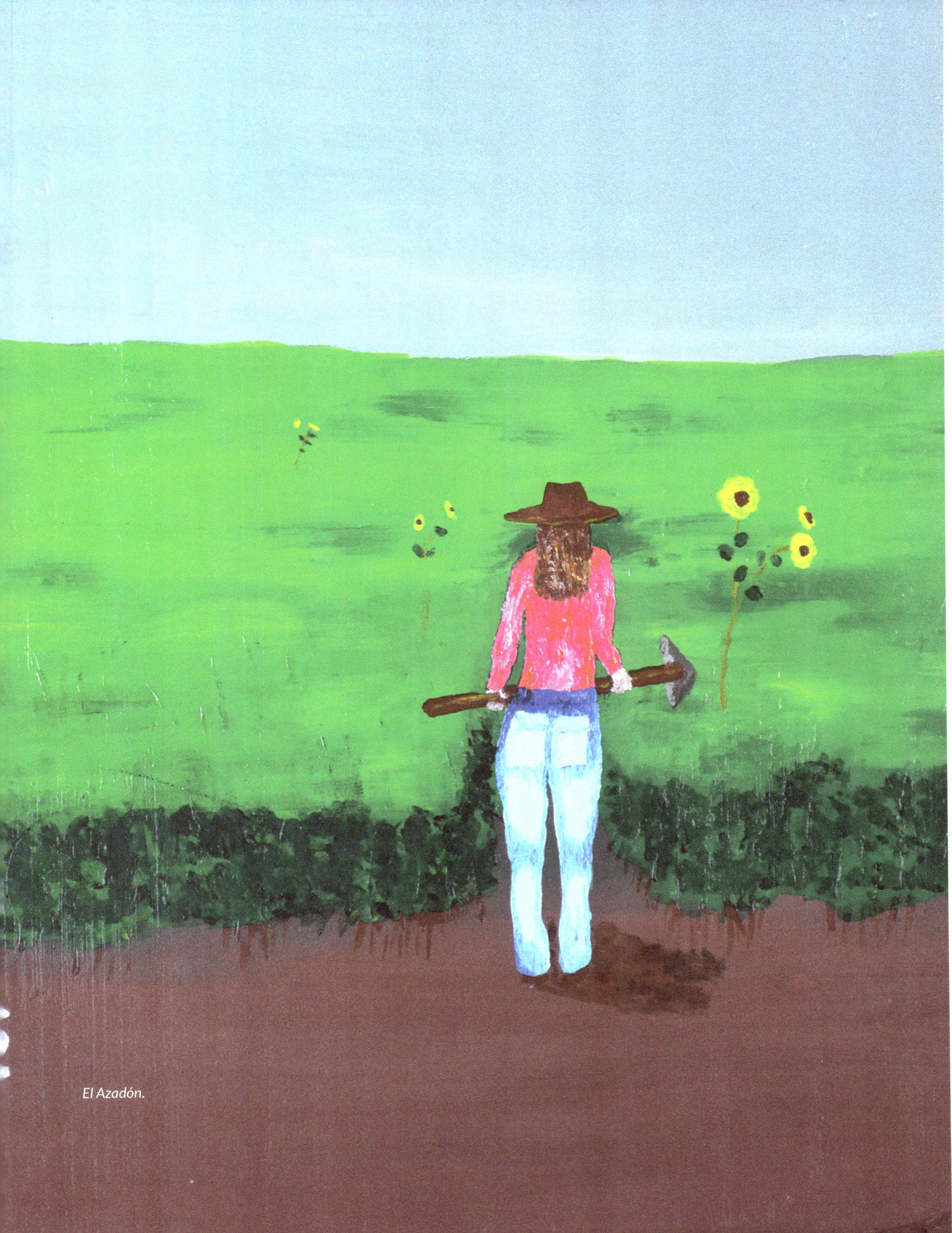

El Azadón.

La matanza (the slaughter)

In Spanish-speaking areas of the world the traditional and ritualistic sacrifice and butchering of livestock such as pigs, cattle, and goats is called la matanza.

Most people do not give much thought to pigs, but they have been an important source of food for humans throughout history. Native to Europe and Africa, they have been domesticated and introduced to almost all areas on Earth where humans inhabit. Pigs were introduced to the Americas by the Spanish explorers at various times during the early colonization.

In Spanish-speaking areas of the world the traditional and ritualistic sacrifice and butchering of livestock such as pigs, cattle, and goats is called *la matanza*. Although there are slight differences in the sacrifice and butchering of pigs in different areas of the Americas, the same basic techniques are used.

In the mid to late 1900s in Edroy and most communities in South Texas, many Tejano families raised a few pigs on their small lots for the *matanza* in winter. In our family, the *matanza* was directed by older, more experienced family members although all members, no matter the age, provided continual and relentless input as to how the ritual can be performed better, either that year or the next.

In the early morning of the *matanza*, and prior to sacrificing the pig, *Papi* took the young children either behind or into the house to keep them from witnessing the scene. *Papi* was an animal lover. I still remember looking at his eyes as we heard the last squeals of the pig. His eyes were always teary, and he looked so sad. He always said, "*pobrecito animal* (poor animal)."

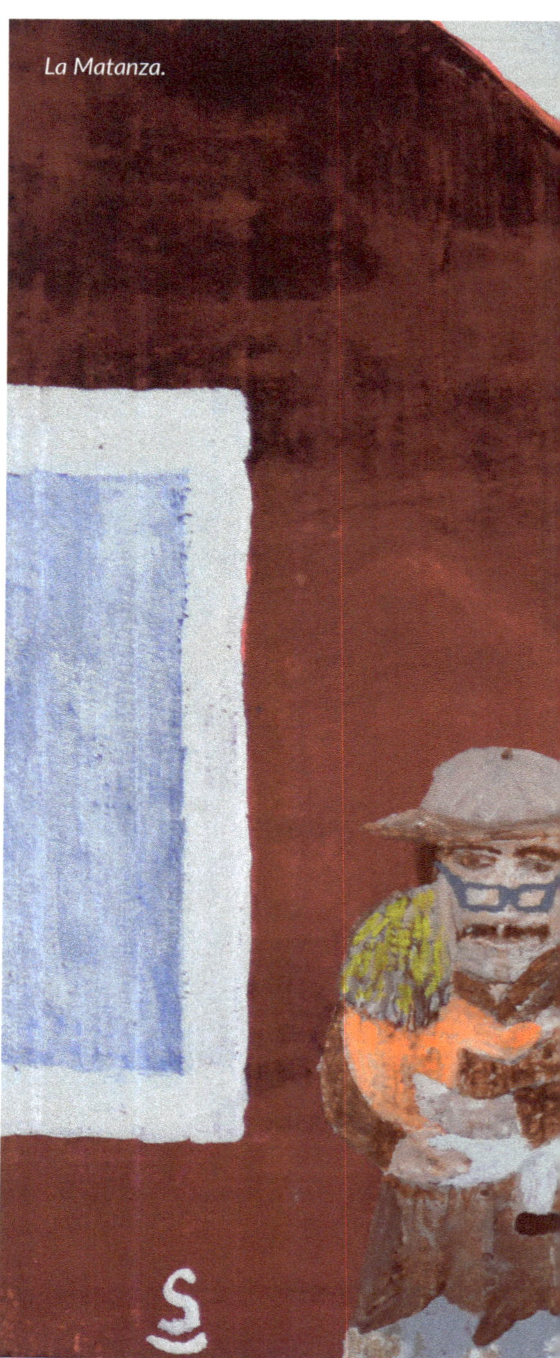

La Matanza.

Other family members captured and subdued the pig. It was quickly and humanely sacrificed usually with a heart puncture. *La sangre* (the blood) was collected to make a delicacy later. One of the more delectable products was making *chicharrones* (cracklings). *Papi* took the lead in butchering the pig, it was one of the ways he fed his family. §

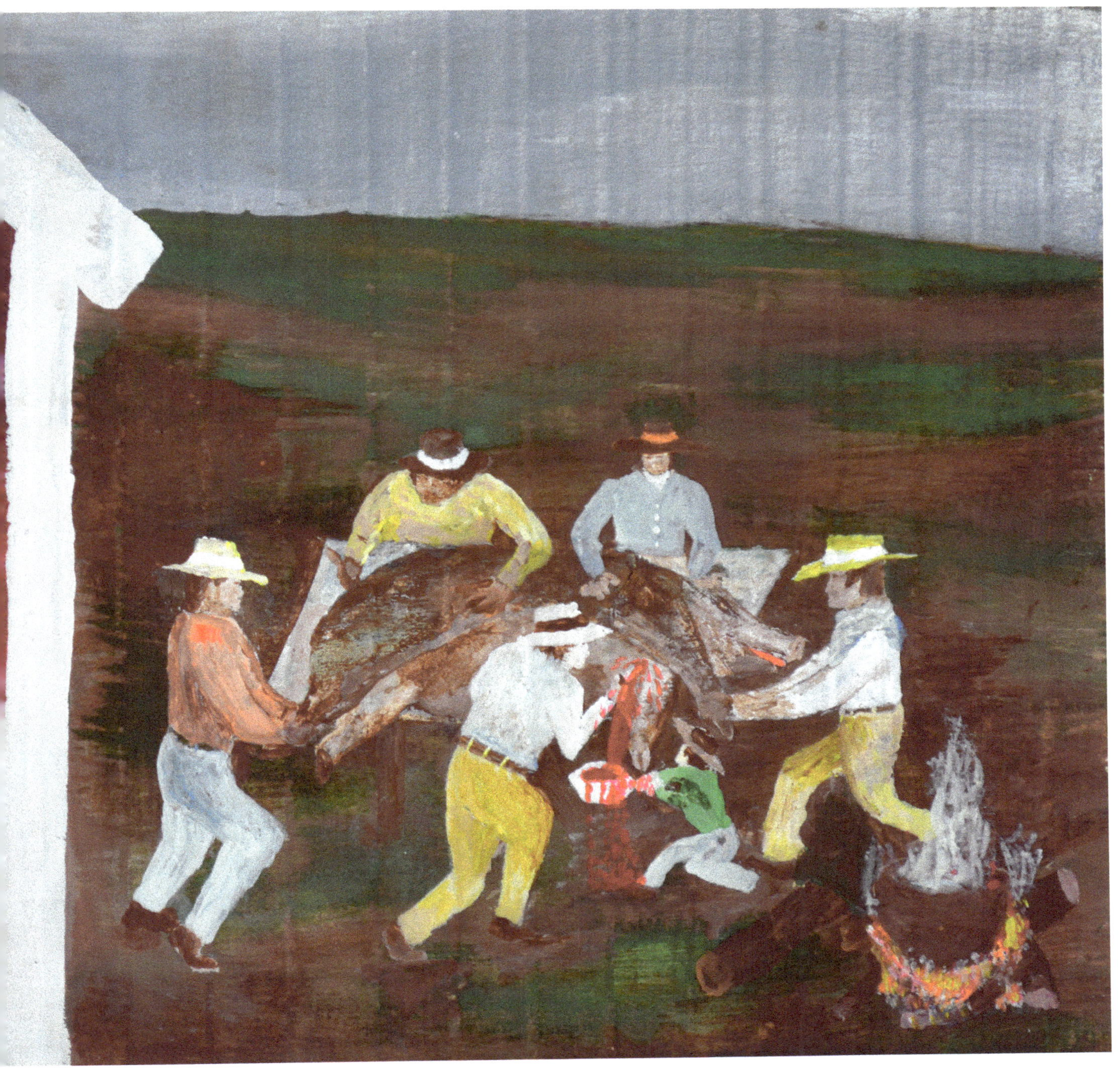

El queso (the cheese)

Papi was a hard-working and proud man. *Mami* was resourceful. My father and his family were almost always employed but occasionally he was not. In the 1980s, he lost his job *en el* pipeline and had to take other jobs like making barns, hoeing the fields, selling watermelons, roofing, plumbing, and carpentry. However, these jobs did not provide a steady source of income.

Papi was adamant against *Mami* applying for government assistance (food stamps). However, and unbeknown to *Papi*, she applied when we needed it.

We received food stamps at least twice during my upbringing.

Papi had a different and more accepting view about government cheese or as some Tejanos called it *queso del condado* (cheese from the county). Although the cheese was part of the Federal commodities program, it was distributed by the county, thus the name.

Papi knew how good my *Mami*'s enchiladas tasted using this cheese. Tasting these enchiladas would certainly change political viewpoints about government assistance in the United States.

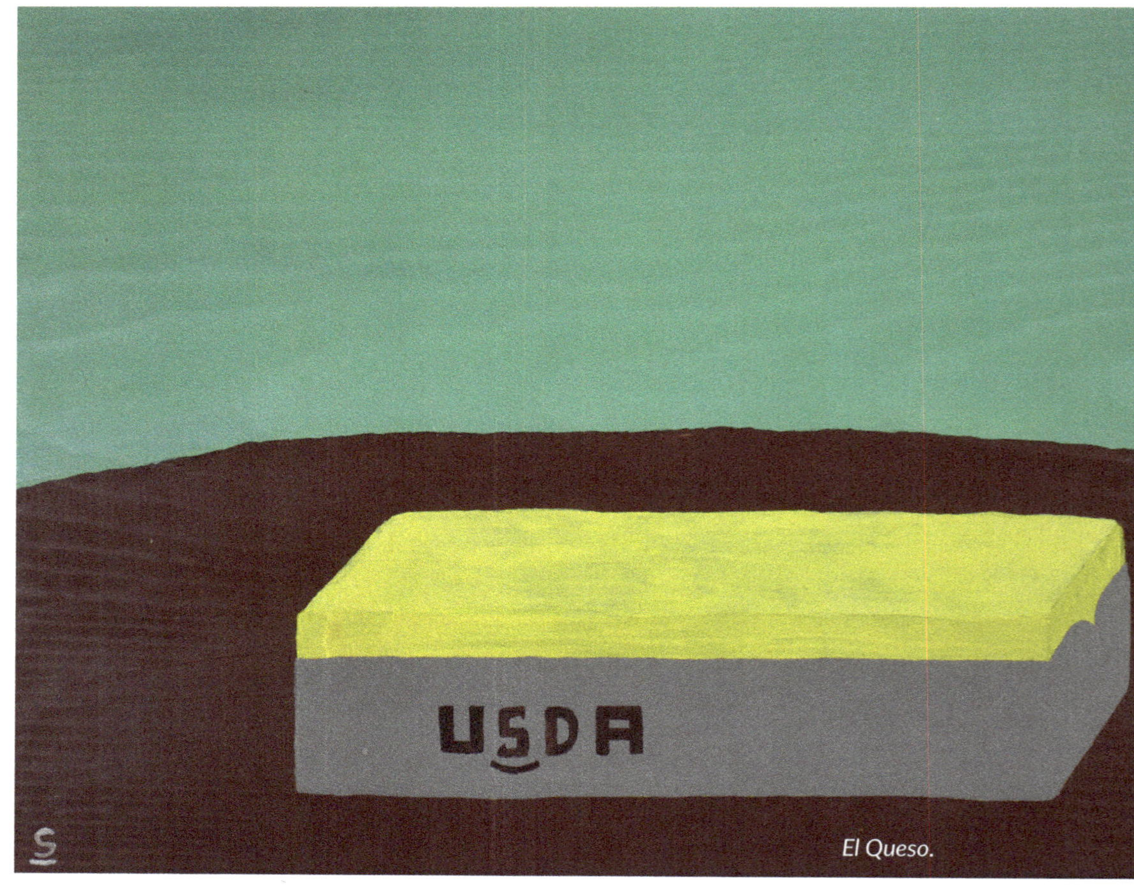

El Queso.

Conclusion: The Alamo

For centuries, Tejanos have lived, raised their families, and died in Texas. They were the first vaqueros, and they worked clearing land for farming (*desenraizería*). Tejanos work in the pipeline and oil industry. They make the best tortillas and really good enchiladas. Some ate cow lungs and still eat pig's blood. They work in grain elevators, cotton gins, and feedlots.

Tejanos hoed fields and picked cotton by hand. They picked watermelons and corn from fields. Tejanos cut their kids hair. Some Tejanos fell in love in high school and eloped. They installed the first indoor toilet in their houses.

Many Tejanos get assigned a nickname. Some have to hitchhike home after football practice. Tejanos were refused service at restaurants.

Finally, this Tejano writes a book to help both father and son better communicate and understand the difficulties of growing up in this rapidly changing world.

Tejanos have historically been under appreciated for their role in shaping Texas. The Alamo is the icon of Texas History yet Tejanos have not been properly acknowledged in their contribution to the Alamo and other significant events in Texas History. For example, few people know that Tejanos and Native Americans built the Alamo and that Tejanos died inside the Alamo.

The dust will not settle over Texas until we "remember the Alamo" with a more accurate and responsible understanding of the significant contribution of Tejanos in history. §

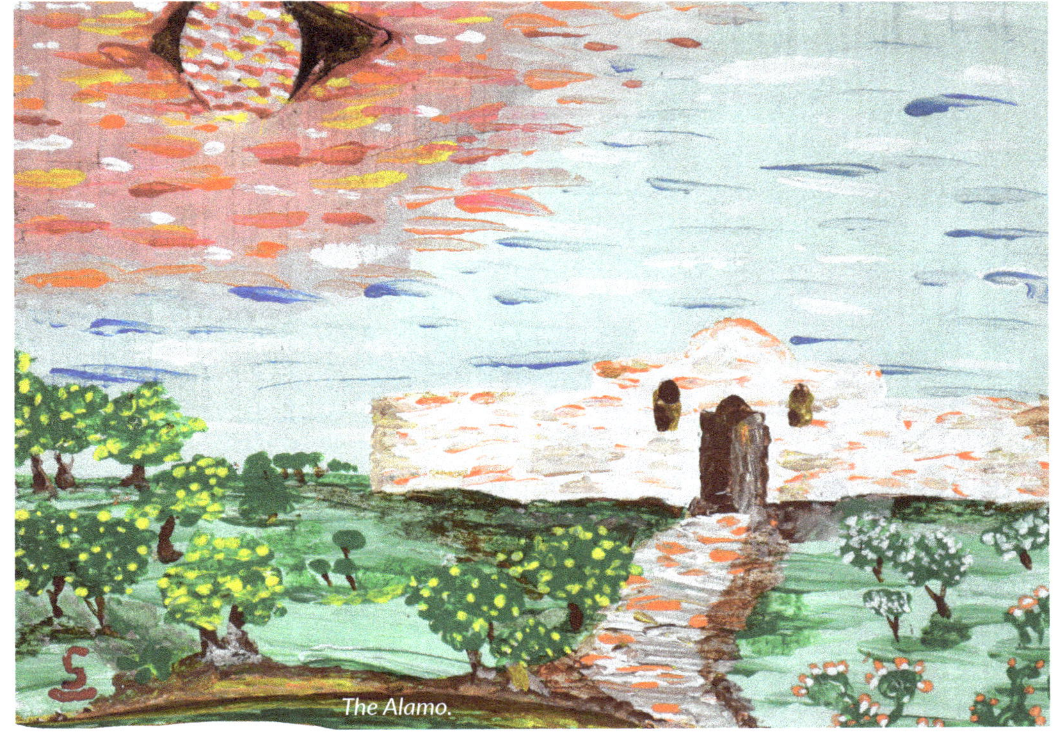

The Alamo.

9 780996 747318